HONGKONGERS' FIGHT FOR FREEDOM

Studies in Critical Social Sciences Book Series

Haymarket Books is proud to be working with Brill Academic Publishers (www.brill.nl) to republish the *Studies in Critical Social Sciences* book series in paperback editions. This peer-reviewed book series offers insights into our current reality by exploring the content and consequences of power relationships under capitalism, and by considering the spaces of opposition and resistance to these changes that have been defining our new age. Our full catalog of *SCSS* volumes can be viewed at https://www.haymarketbooks .org/series_collections/4-studies-in-critical-social-sciences.

HONGKONGERS' FIGHT FOR FREEDOM

Voices from the 2019 Anti-extradition Movement

NAM KIU TSING

Haymarket Books
Chicago, IL

First published in 2023 by Brill Academic Publishers, The Netherlands
© 2023 Koninklijke Brill NV, Leiden, The Netherlands

Published in paperback in 2024 by
Haymarket Books
P.O. Box 180165
Chicago, IL 60618
773-583-7884
www.haymarketbooks.org

ISBN: 979-8-88890-239-4

Distributed to the trade in the US through Consortium Book Sales and
Distribution (www.cbsd.com) and internationally through Ingram Publisher
Services International (www.ingramcontent.com).

This book was published with the generous support of Lannan Foundation,
Wallace Action Fund, and the Marguerite Casey Foundation.

Special discounts are available for bulk purchases by organizations and
institutions. Please call 773-583-7884 or email info@haymarketbooks.org for more
information.

Cover design by Jamie Kerry and Ragina Johnson.

Printed in the United States.

Library of Congress Cataloging-in-Publication data is available.

Contents

Preface

An ailment cannot be cured without the right antidote. Peaceful assemblies and protest marches which had become common occurrences in Hong Kong rapidly deteriorated into unresolvable violent confrontations in the autumn of 2019. Social dignitaries, both local and abroad, repeatedly urged the Hong Kong SAR (Special Administrative Region) government to resolve the matter through political means. The most broadly accepted proposal among them was to set up an independent commission of inquiry[1] to investigate how the incident (initially the June 12 Incident, but later expanded to include similar ones that followed) happened and whether the police had used excessive force, and to suggest ways to ameliorate the situation to prevent similar incidents from happening etc.

Police tactics used against the protesters on 12 June 2019 were widely criticised for the disproportionate use of force on peaceful protests, causing numerous injuries (one person was shot in the eye). Moreover, their dispersal strategy had almost led to a fatal stampede.[2] From that day on, calls for setting up an independent inquiry commission came from numerous quarters, from the former Chief Judge of the Court of Final Appeal, former high officials, holders of public office, to international human rights leaders, all of whom agreed that an independent inquiry was a feasible solution to the political crisis at hand. However, not only did the police oppose this vehemently, but they intensified their suppression, thereby exacerbating the conflict.

With no hope for an independent public inquiry in the foreseeable future, some civil groups nevertheless strived to provide alternative reports.[3] Joining this effort, a group of us – academics, mindful of civil society's need to reveal

---

1   See Hong Kong Public Opinion Research Institute, "80% of those interviewed supported setting up an independent commission of inquiry to investigate police's use of force", reported in *Hong Kong 01*, 15 Nov 2019 https://bit.ly/3OYWLGj (in Chinese, last viewed 1 Oct 2022).

2   On that afternoon, the Civil Human Rights Front organised a mass meeting outside Citic Tower on Lung Wui Road. The police tried to disperse the crowds by advancing westwards from Legislative Council Road on the left, while firing at least ten tear gas shots. Nearly a hundred panicking protesters tried to escape by thronging into Citic Tower, nearly causing a fatal stampede. See: "Tear gas attack at Citic Tower nearly causing fatal stampede", *Apple Daily*, 19 June 2019 https://bit.ly/3Pz5Zt1 (in Chinese, no longer available) See also "[Independent Police Complaints Council] Narrow escape from fatal stampede in Citic Tower, Call for police review on use of tear gas", *Hong Kong 01*, 16 May 2020 https://bit.ly/3c2MQ4a (in Chinese) (last viewed 31 Aug 2022).

3   Not blessed by legal powers for investigation, and with limited resources, they still tried to pursue various themes according to their respective concerns and expertise. Regarding analyses of police law enforcement, there are: "How Not to Police a Protest: Unlawful Use of Force by Hong

the voices of the participants, group together to study what had transpired from the perspective of the participants. Lacking adequate resources, we nevertheless hoped to contribute to public understanding of this protest movement. Through in-depth interviews, we hoped to access participants' perspectives, experiences, thoughts, worries, judgments, hopes and imaginations, and from these, the reasons and motives behind their participation, their changing actions and roles, organisational patterns, and strategies, down to their feelings, expectations, reflections, etc. For individual interviewees, their experiences and thoughts make up part of certain episodes in their lives, and these, in turn, are snippets of "micro histories" of Hong Kong society. As components of society's "macro history", these snippets, when organised and analysed, might enable us to see the big picture, and to better understand the Movement itself: how it had grown to such a scale with broad participation, and how it had managed to sustain itself for such a long stretch of time. The 2019 Anti-Extradition Law Amendment Bill (Anti-ELAB) Movement in Hong Kong is certainly an important turning point in contemporary Chinese politics and historical development, as in international politics. In our interviews, we tried to provide a temporary but safe and trustful context in which the participants could, through their interaction with the interviewer, reconstruct the meaning of their participation in this Movement. This meaning pertains to their personal lives, but it also provides, at the same time, a concrete and grounded anchor for macro, political-historical writing.

Our team is made up of ten persons, who normally split up into two-person sub-teams. The 56 in-depth interviews were conducted with a common interview framework. Each interview targeted one interviewee and was conducted in a private context conducive to uninhibited conversation. To maximise protection for us and our informants, we refrained from disclosing our real names

---

Kong Police" by Amnesty International https://www.amnesty.org/en/documents/asa17/0576 /2019/en/ (published in June 2019, last viewed 31 Aug 2022). "Silencing Millions: Unchecked Violence of Internationally Recognized Human Rights by the Hong Kong Police Force" by the Progressive Scholars Group https://www.docdroid.net/0EA2Bhy/silencingmillions-text-final -pdf, (published in 2020, last viewed 31 Aug 2022), (A group of local professionals, 2019, no longer available). Surveys on public sentiment and participants' stance: "Anti-extradition Bill Movement: People's Public Sentiment Report" by the Hong Kong Public Opinion Research Institute https://www.pori.hk/wp-content/uploads/2021/01/pcf_s3_ppt_v2_bilingual_cty.pdf, (published on 13 Dec 2019, last viewed 31 Aug 2022), and Centre for Communication and Public Opinion Survey, The Chinese University of Hong Kong. (May 2020). *Research Report on Public Opinion During the Anti-Extradition Bill (Fugitive Offenders Bill) Movement in Hong Kong.* http://www.com.cuhk.edu.hk/ccpos/en/pdf/202005PublicOpinionSurveyReport-ENG .pdf, (last viewed 9 Jan 2023) etc. Apart from these, book compilations of news reports as well as academic research are gradually emerging.

here except for one of the authors, Nam Kiu Tsing, a retired professor who is now residing in Taiwan, and who represents the writing team to publish this work. We also protect our informants' identity, having not asked for their real names and identifying them only by pseudonyms. The recorded interviews were transcribed by trusted persons, and these transcriptions made up the main body of the writing. Before the interviews took place, the participants were requested to fill out a simple questionnaire (no names required), which recorded certain background information. In our report below, some of the personal characteristics of our participants, including their genders, are jumbled, to avoid identification.

1   Brief Profile of Interviewees

The 56 interviewees were recruited through the social networks of our team members, and the interviews were done between October and December of 2019. The gender ratio (males to females) is 34:22. In terms of age, more than half of them (30) were under 29, with six of them aged 15 to 19, twenty-two of them aged 30 to 49, and four over 50 years of age. The oldest among them (two) were aged 60, one of whom being a member of "Protect Our Kids Campaign", a group composed of middle-aged to senior citizens, founded to help frontline protesters. Most of the interviewees were employed (39), and the other thirteen were secondary or college students. The educational level of our participants was generally quite high: more than half (35) had qualifications at university or above, with nine among these reaching post-graduate levels. This relatively high education level might be related to the social network of the research team members. However, this was also evident in another research (Lee et al., 2019). The reason given was that tertiary education had expanded significantly in the past 20 years, and many of the participants in the Movement were drawn from the younger age groups (Lee et al., 2019, p. 12). In our own research, among the twelve full-time students, five were secondary students, seven were university/college students, and one post-graduate student.

In-depth interviews allow us to explore the subjectivities of our participants in a relatively short time: their motivations and what drove them to join the Movement, changes in their thoughts or emotions during participation, and their views and expectations in relation to the socio-political environment. Most of the interviews were single occasions, lasting on average an hour or more. One of our participants, however, was interviewed three times, each lasting almost one and a half hours. In-depth interviews required trust between the interviewer and the interviewee, and this was clearly forthcoming in our interviews. Our promise of anonymity obviously contributed to their willing-ness to talk, but many of them also took this interview to be a treasured oppor-tunity to process their profound experiences in those months.

Our interviewees played a wide range of roles in the Movement. The most frequently taken-up role is "Supplies transport and provision", "Sentinel" and "Publicity materials". Among our interviewees, those on the forefront were, namely, *"chung chung ji"* (衝衝子 in Chinese, protester positioned to charge forward), and "magician" (protester who tries to forestall police advance by throwing homemade firebombs). Many of our interviewees took up multiple roles, and these also varied according to changing situations and needs in the Movement. Personal experience might also come into play, such as when some of our interviewees were arrested, they would retreat temporarily, or take up a more back-seat position to avoid being arrested again.

Zooming into our interviewees' experiences and situations in the Movement, 46 of them had "gobbled tear gas", 22 had been injured on the spot, and 12 had been arrested. We would imagine that having been arrested or injured would leave a physical or psychological mark of some sort, but we discovered that such a mark could be rather deep even for those who had "gobbled tear gas". This experience could significantly change their views and feelings towards the regime or the social movement.

The above is only a brief sketch of the background of our interviewees, based on a simple questionnaire. In what follows, we shall draw on our interview data to dig deeper into the motives, goals, values, and feelings of the participants, in order to better understand their subjectivities which, in turn, might shed light on the motivating force behind the Movement and its characteristics. History always has its specific context and social factors, all of which are above and beyond the wishes or capacities of individuals. On the other hand, the val-ues, wishes and even feelings of individuals do impact on the characteristics and direction of social movements. At this point of time, we do not know how much and in what ways these individuals' subjectivities impact on the unfold-ing of history. But we do believe that since they have occurred at this juncture, they would certainly have left an imprint. We hope that, through this study, we could preserve and present this imprint.

A brief note about the sources drawn on in the following presentation is in order here. Readers would discover that some of the newspaper and other resources we indicate in the footnotes are no longer available online. This is not due to normal volatility of internet resources, but because of the govern-ment clampdown on newspapers and social media in the name of "national security" since 2020. The curtailment of the freedom of expression is obvious in this, as in the forced anonymity of most of our authors.

Acknowledgements

We would like to express our utmost gratitude to the 56 interviewees in this study. Their courage, trust, and generosity in sharing their stories during those months of fear, anger and sadness is highly admirable. A few of them have perhaps left for foreign lands, forced to forsake the beloved city they have fought for. Perhaps some of them are now behind bars, sacrificing their freedom for their vision of a better place they call home.

Our thanks are also due to writers and media workers whose work we have drawn on in this report. In particular, many of the local journalists among them have produced excellent works which succeed to inscribe in history what has transpired in that fateful year of 2019, despite the strenuous efforts of those in power to cover up, distort and eliminate the truth. Some of these journalists, as we know, are now incarcerated for nothing other than having made an outstanding contribution to independent and critical reporting and analysis, which are, sadly, no longer tolerated in Hong Kong.

We are also mindful of those, in this part of the world and elsewhere, who are jailed, injured, in exile or just trying to live a normal life at home or abroad, doing whatever they could to keep up hope for a better future. The strength of faith they manifest is inspiring for all of us in this age of despondency and confusion.

Author Statement

While I am credited as the author of this book, the true authors are a team of Hong Kong scholars and researchers. In the eyes of the Chinese and Hong Kong governments, the contents of this book violate the Hong Kong National Security Law(NSL) – possible charges include secession, subversion, terrorism, etc. When publishing children's fables is "guilty of sedition" according to designated NSL judges, the authors of this book – who document and disseminate the voices of dissidents – face unfathomable risk. To protect the personal safety of the authors, they must remain anonymous. This is the reality of Hong Kong today, when academic freedom and freedom of speech no longer exist.

However, someone must represent the authors during the publication process to correspond with the publisher and sign the contract. Bestowed with the trust of the writing team, I am honored to take on this role even though I only took a small part in the book project.

Heartfelt thanks to David Fasenfest, Series Editor of Studies in Critical Social Sciences, for bringing this book into the world. All credit of this book goes to the anonymous authors and interviewees. Glory to Hong Kong.

Nam Kiu Tsing
November, 2022

Figures

CHAPTER 1

The Prelude

1 The Story of a Secondary School Student

We begin this book by the story of a secondary school student, Streambreaker,[1] who participated in the 2019 Anti-ELAB Movement, the first time he joined a protest against the government. Streambreaker joined the march on June 9th. After getting pepper-sprayed by the riot police when he was running away from being arrested, Streambreaker changed from being a PRN (peaceful, rational, non-violent) to being "valiant". Like many Hong Kong young protesters, he then tried to join every rally and march, stopping cars, moving objects and road fences and so on to set up road blockades. Yet he did not feel comfortable with throwing bricks. On July 27th, the police fired many bullets. He protected himself with a shield made of cardboard and plastic bottles and began to throw plastic bottles. After getting hit by a sponge bullet, someone picked him up and took him to the hospital. He lied to the medical staff that he got injured when playing football. In the march on August 25th, he was arrested and locked up for 2 days. After his arrest, he still joined marches or rallies, though he became more careful. He said that he would only be "running from places to places, doing things like throwing back tear gas (canisters)."

When the government used the "Emergency Regulations Ordinance" to announce the "Anti-Mask Law" on October 4th, Streambreaker immediately took action to protest. "The following day in the afternoon on Saturday (October 5th). ... Alone I wore a black mask, covering the right eye,[2] sat down at one of the underground stations (all underground stations were blocked), and raised my hand with the 'Five Demands'[3] gesture. ... then people started to

---

1 Normally we asked our interviewees to choose their own pseudonyms. This seventeen-year-old schoolboy chose the nickname of a villainy character in a Hong Kong comedy-film, *Love on Delivery* (1994)：Tuen-Shui-Lau (literally, someone who breaks the flow of the stream) the Senior Fellow (斷水流大師兄 in Chinese). This character in the film is a veteran karate fighter who uses despicable means to win over the girlfriend of the major character. In this book, we call this interviewee Streambreaker.

2 This is an allusion to an incident in the evening of 11th August 2019. A young woman who was a volunteer first-aider got shot by a bean-bag round in her right eye, allegedly by the police. The police never admitted this, and the young woman lost her judicial review against the police, who had obtained her medical records from the hospital without notifying her.

3 The Five Demands were put up by protesters in mid-June of 2019. See later paragraphs.

give me food and water, even bubble tea! (laugh)" Streambreaker was arrested again by riot police in December when he did not run fast enough to escape from a protest scene.

Why did he still go out after his first arrest? Was he not afraid to be arrested again? He replied, "First I had no home to return to (left home following a fight with his parents after he came out on bail). Second, I said before that I would go whenever there was a rally or march. I wanted to keep the promise ... a 'self-imposed rule' so to speak, like I set down rules to study for how many hours." He kept explaining, "There is a motto: 'Born in a time of chaos, one has a responsibility'".

Hong Kong society was entirely changed in 2019. After this year, none of its citizens including Streambreaker could recognise their own society. Their lives were also no longer the same as before. Everyone became an alien in his or her own homeland. What is left to us are the very precious voices of the people who have participated in making their own history, which, tragically, is leading to an opposite direction to what they had fought for. Some of them are now in prison, some facing trial in court, some were charged, and some in exile – all these originated from the 2019 Anti-ELAB Movement, which marked the turning point in Hong Kong history. In February 2019, the Government of the Hong Kong Special Administrative Region (HKSAR) presented to the Legislative Council an amendment bill pertaining to the extradition law,[4] which, once passed, would allow extradition of fugitives in Hong Kong to Mainland China, Taiwan, and Macao. Opposition to the amendment gathered force, and the SAR government subsequently put the amendment bill on hold. Despite this, intensifying political differences and massive mobilisation, which, in turn, was fuelled by ruthless police suppression, rapidly attracted media attention, and the 2019 Anti-ELAB Movement soon landed in the international limelight. The landslide victory of the opposition camp in the District Council elections in November 2019 signified majority support for the Movement. Yet, the SAR government made no move to ameliorate the situation, not to say to reach out to the opposition, even in the smallest way. Worse still, Beijing promulgated, in phenomenal speed in the summer of 2020, the Hong Kong National Security

---

4   This was the *Fugitive Offenders and Mutual Legal Assistance in Criminal Matters (Amendment) Bill 2019*, commonly referred to as the Extradition Law Amendment Bill. This involves amendments to the *Fugitives Offenders Ordinance (cap 503)* and *Mutual Legal Assistance in Criminal Matters Ordinance (cap 525)*. For details of the Amendment Bill, please refer to Lam Tai-Fai, "Brief Notes by the Bar Association, 24 Q&As related to the Amendment Bill", *Hong Kong 01*, 6 June 2019 (in Chinese). https://bit.ly/2X7q7eo (in Chinese, last viewed 3 Sept 2022).

Law, the draconian power of which ushered Hong Kong into a completely new era, with unprecedented challenges.

Back to the early stages of the proposal of the Extradition Law Amendment Bill, that is, from March to May 2019, civil groups as well as pan-democratic Legislative Councillors organised several anti-extradition protests. These were not well-attended, with participation figures ranging only from a few hundred to a thousand, to at most 130,000.[5] With heightened public discussion, however, the Government decided, in late May, to bypass the normal process of scrutiny in the Bills Committee and, instead, to bring the Amendment Bill directly for its second reading in full Council on June 12th. This attempt on the part of the SAR Government to accelerate the process led to heightened mobilisation by opposition groups. Among these, the Civil Human Rights Front (CHRF) called for a peaceful protest march on June 9th, which attracted, according to their estimation, over 1 million people. The SAR Government, however, stood its ground. Even while the crowds were still dispersing late that night, the government spokesperson announced that the second reading of the Amendment Bill would go on as scheduled on June 12th. In the late evening of June 11th, people began to gather in the vicinity of the Government Headquarters and the Legislative Council in Central and Admiralty, purportedly trying to stop the legislating process the next day.

Starting from the early morning of June 12th, groups of protesters took to the streets outside the Legislative Council. The police took action in the afternoon, firing hundreds of bullets of various kinds, injuring more than 80 people.[6] The Commissioner of Police, Stephen Lo Wai-chung, even designated the protests as "riot", and subsequently five protesters were arrested for rioting. The confrontation escalated, and CHRF called for another protest rally on June 16th, hoping to add pressure on the Government. The Chief Executive (CE) Carrie Lam announced the suspension of the Amendment Bill, but refused to withdraw it, nor to answer to the other requests put forth by the protesters.

---

5 Police estimation of participation in protests usually fell much below that of the organisers. For example, for the marches on 29 April and 29 June, police figures were 22,800 and 338,000 respectively, while those announced by the organiser, Civil Human Rights Front (CHRF), were 130,000 and 1,030,000 respectively.

6 The police announced that they had fired more than 240 rounds of tear gas, about 3 rounds of bean-bag bullets, about 19 rounds of rubber bullets and about 30 rounds of sponge grenades. There were more than 80 casualties, with quite a few of them having sustained head injuries, including one who was shot in the eye. See "Police admitted using tear gas which were past 'Best Use Before' period; no danger posed", https://web.archive.org/web/2019091 4011902/https:/news.rthk.hk/rthk/ch/component/k2/1474222-20190812.htm RTHK radio website, 13 Sept 2019, (in Chinese, last viewed 3 Sept 2022).

The protest march went on as scheduled on June 16th, with an unprecedented turnout of 2 million, according to the organiser's estimation. By then the protesters had concretised their so-called "Five Demands": (1) Withdraw the Extradition Amendment Bill;[7] (2) Retract the designation of the protests as "riot"; (3) Amnesty for the arrested protesters; (4) Establish an independent committee of inquiry into police brutality; and (5) The CE, Carrie Lam, to step down from office. Later, the fifth demand was replaced by "Dual Universal Suffrage", i.e., free and fair elections for both the Legislative Councillors and the CE. Researchers point out that the emergence of the "Five Demands" made two things clear. Firstly, the drastic elevation of police suppression on June 12th made "police brutality" a new and important concern of the Anti-Extradition Movement, and as police violence intensified, the Movement dragged on and became increasingly radicalised (Stott et al., 2020, p. 826; Lee et al., 2019, p. 16). Secondly, with the "Five Demands", the Movement shifted from a single-issue protest movement focusing on the Amendment of the Extradition Laws to a broad quest for democratic revamping of the political structure as a whole (Lee et al., 2019, p. 17).

From then on, the protest movement went on for more than half a year, as the government refused to budge, and confrontations intensified. Significant incidents include protesters' siege of Police Headquarters in Wanchai on June 21st; storming into the Legislative Council on July 1st, with selected symbols of official power being damaged or disfigured; protesters marching onto the Central People's Government Liaison Office and disfiguring the national emblem on the entrance on July 21st; and the atrocious attack by dozens of men in white T-shirts, suspected to have close links with triad societies, on passers-by later the same day in Yuen Long. Armed with wooden staffs and rattan canes, these men wantonly attacked people they saw in the station and in the carriages. Curiously, warnings of the attack had been widely circulated before it happened, and when it did, numerous calls for help to the police were made. The police not only had ignored the alert beforehand, but they were found to arrive at the scene 39 minutes after receiving the first report from the public. By that time, the perpetrators had already left. Dubbed "the 7.21 Incident",[8] this occurrence as well as police reaction (or, non-reaction) shocked and disappointed the public.

---

7   The Government eventually withdrew the Amendment Bill on 4th September 2019, but by then the focus of the protests had already shifted to police brutality and unjust law enforcement.

8   For details of the 7.21 Incident, please refer to "Re-assembling the Facts of the Indiscriminate Attack Incident in Yuen Long: Police arrived one minute after the White-Clad Men departed", *Initium Media*, 23 July 2019 https://theinitium.com/article/20190723-hongk ong-yuenlong-incident-timeline/ (last viewed, 3 Sept 2022). For later developments,

Together with the escalation of police suppression, this added fuel to the movement. Large-scale protests occurred every weekend thereafter, followed by violent clashes between police and protesters, and mass arrests. In August, protesters also called for city-wide strikes and blockage of the airport. In the late night of August 31st, a dispute over political views broke out among a few passengers in Prince Edward metro station. Riot police and the "Raptors"[9] were sent in, emerging in the carriages at a different platform, clubbing the passengers indiscriminately with batons and attacking them with pepper spray. They also closed the station, refusing entry for the press and first aid personnel. Known subsequently as the 831 Incident,[10] this gave rise to widely circulated rumours that there were indeed deaths in the station that night. The slogan "7.21, no police to be seen! 8.31, (police) beat people to death!" quickly became popular, and the torn relationship between civilians and the police was beyond repair. Frequent protests went on in subsequent months, and street confrontations exacerbated, as the government continued its policy of violent repression, dubbed the "Stop Violence and Curb Disorder" tactic, refusing to ameliorate the situation through political means.

Intensification of suppression led to more rampant confrontation on the streets. In just the month of November that year, the police laid siege to the Chinese University of Hong Kong and the Polytechnic University of Hong

---

please see "Protests in Hong Kong: Hong Kong Police arrested pan-democrat Councillor, re-igniting the argument over the Yuen Long 7.21 Incident" https://www.bbc.com/zhong wen/trad/chinese-news-53919228.amp (in Chinese, last viewed 3 Sept 2022). See also an award-winning TV news story, "7.21: Who Speaks the Truth?", *Hong Kong Connection*, RTHK, screened on 13 July 2020: https://www.youtube.com/watch?v=or4B7NpHwbY, (no longer available). A second report made with newly-found sources is: "Pursuing the 7.21 Incident Further: Tracking Suspicious Propaganda Materials; Traces Picked up via Freeze-Frame" *Standnews*, 20 July 2021 https://bit.ly/3Is6ZfT (no longer available). A third video report was made on the third anniversary of the Incident: "[3rd Anniversary of 7.21] Independent reporters insist on reporting: [The Unfinished Case of 7.21]", *Radio Free Asia*, 20 Jul 2022 (in Chinese), https://www.rfa.org/cantonese/news/htm/hk-7.21-07202022062402.html (last viewed 3 Sept 2022).

9   This is the Special Tactical Contingent, known commonly as the Raptors, or Elite Team. They were regularly seen on the protest spots in 2019.

10   For the 8.31 Incident, please refer to: "What happened inside Prince Edward MTR Station on the night of 8.31? Reconstituting the indiscriminate police attack on passengers", *Initium Media*, 5 Sept 2019. https://theinitium.com/article/20190905-hongk ong-prince-edward-mtr-station-police/. (in Chinese, last viewed 3 Sept 2022). See also "First Anniversary of 8.31, Litigant in the Admiralty Station Incident, Leung Yiu Ting, says: Argument over whether anybody had died misses the point. He will demand civil claims from the police", Hong Kong Citizen News, 30 Aug 2020. https://hkcnews.com/arti cle/33370/8.31 (in Chinese, no longer available).

Kong consecutively, firing up to 5,000 and 11,000 rounds of various bullets respectively, which made up more than half of the total shots fired in the second half of the year.[11] It was only in late January 2020, with the COVID19 pandemic, and the SAR government imposing a social distancing ban on public gatherings that mass protest activities disappeared. But from then on, Hong Kong will never be the same.

In Part 1 of this book, we shall present a general account drawn from our interviews of participants in the 2019 Movement. Major themes include why they entered the Movement in the first place, how the Movement evolved and how the roles of the protesters changed and diversified as the Movement intensified. We shall also describe the "Be Water" mode of resistance as chosen and experienced by our interviewees, and the sense of community and local identity which both underlay the Movement and was constructed in its progress. Part Two contains the stories as told by five of our interviewees, drawn from different age groups and positions in the Movement. These stories enable us to access the thoughts and emotions of the individuals – the "human face", so to speak, behind this massive resistance. The book ends with a last chapter, "Lessons from Hong Kong", which attempts to put the 2019 Movement in its historical context: the changed face of Hong Kong post-2019, the broken promise of democracy since 1997, the emergence of protest culture from 2003 onwards, and the place of the 2019 Movement in China's changing relationship with the world. Last but not the least, we make a case for the weight of stories in history. Hong Kong as we knew it might be no more, but memories and stories will remain. This work is an attempt to help preserve them.

---

11   For numbers of fired shots, please refer to: "The Movement into its half year: Police fired nearly 30,000 shots, one third into PolyU, Said to be akin to military operation", *Radio France Internationale* (Chinese broadcast), 10 Dec 2019. https://bit.ly/3aqeUhs (in Chinese, last viewed 3 Sept 2022).

PART 1

The Study

∴

CHAPTER 2

Motivations for Participation

1   To Stop the Amendments

Most of the participants in the 2019 Movement aimed at stopping the Extradition Law amendments, with a deep political fear that the Central Government in Beijing would intervene into the legal system of Hong Kong and constrain the freedom of the society. Among those interviewed, however, few were aware of the potential impact of the Extradition Law Amendment Bill when it was first proposed by the government in February 2019. Most of them did not participate in the Movement until the 9th of June, when they observed the obstinacy of the Hong Kong government to pass the Bill and the brutality of the police force in dispersing the protesters.

Grace (Chinese enterprise employee) and Zoe (civil servant) are the two exceptions. With their unusually high political sensitivity, they had participated in the Movement much earlier. Grace said:

> I pay close attention to current affairs and have always followed any new political controversies in Hong Kong. At the time, the average citizen might not have noticed it yet, but a big storm was already stirring up in the political circles
>
> On the 28th of April, the Civil Human Rights Front organised a relatively small-scale march, in which I participated. I closely followed the development of the Bill and helped with spreading the word, to tell my friends the points in the Extradition Bill that warranted attention and alert.

Zoe was also quick to look into the Bill's details together with her friends:

> Upon reflection, I think back in April (2019), I was already aware of the proposal to amend the Fugitive Offenders Ordinance. Luckily there were professionals who know about law to explain to the citizens how the bill would affect us. As I understood more, I realised that the bill was quite a big threat to Hong Kong people. Having gained understanding then, I would participate in almost every march when I could. My motivation was to tell the government that we did not agree with such amendments.

Unlike Grace and Zoe, most other respondents had not participated in any protests against the Bill until the 9th of June. On that day, the Civil Human Rights Front organised another Anti-Extradition Bill march. A series of events preceding the march had already drawn wider public attention to the issue. In May, a bill committee for the Fugitive Offenders Ordinance Amendment Bill was formed by the Legislative Council (LegCo). Chaotic showdowns soon broke out in the LegCo between the pro-establishment and pan-democrats camps over the procedures of chairperson election. As the rival camps eventually elected their own chairpersons, the amendments went into stalemate. On the 20th of May, Secretary for Security John Lee announced that he would bypass the bill committee and submit the bill directly to the LegCo.

Weeks of clashes inside the LegCo combined with the government's unusual means to speed up the amendment heightened tension, and public attention grew. Alarmed at the emergency, civil groups rapidly stepped-up information outreach and mobilisation against the bill. Petitions by Christian groups and university and secondary school alumni groups mushroomed, with some issuing their own statements in the press. The Civil Human Rights Front campaigned for participation at their upcoming June 9 march. Over a million people turned out, way over the organiser's anticipated 300,000. In our interviewees' testimonies, it is clear that they had been aware of the amendments. It was the escalation leading up to the 9th of June that finally prompted them to act:

> [Toward the latter half of Form 5 (Year 11),] the extradition bill was mentioned in my Liberal Studies[1] class ..., so I did know a bit about it. Since there was so much publicity (about the June 9 march), I decided to go. It was my first time .... I deliberated on it: it was reasonable to oppose [the bill]. That's why I went.
>
> Streambreaker, secondary school student

> I first participated on the 9th of June. But I had been paying attention to related news and LegCo discussions. I noticed that the government just kept lying. They had no credibility whatsoever.
>
> Dove, occupation not identified

---

1   "Liberal Studies" was a compulsory school subject for the Diploma of Secondary Education Examination (DSE Exam) introduced in the so-called "Education Reform" in the 2000s and first administered in 2012. Later blamed for having "enticed" youngsters to lawlessness and lack of patriotism after the 2019 Movement, Liberal Studies was revamped, or rather, trimmed, partially rewritten and renamed "Citizenship and Social Development" in 2021.

FIGURE 1   A million people marched. On June 9, 2019, a million people marched in protest
of the ELAB, the first large-scale rally of the time. As protesters passed by the Ta
Kung Pao newspaper office, the TV on the building's curtain wall was screening
the then Chief Executive Carrie Lam's Question-and-Answer session at the
Legislative Council asserting that the bill would not be withdrawn, and a protester
was raising a red Anti-ELAB placard.

I first participated on the 9th of June. But I had been following related
news and LegCo discussions. I found that the government's credibility
[was lacking], or they just kept lying. Their attitude had also been very
bad.

>   AB, self-employed

Many had marched in the hope that the government would respect public
opinion. They expected that once their number reached a certain level, the government would at least take their views into account and make certain concessions. Unfortunately, this expectation was to be crushed that very same night.

2   Anger and Shock Mobilised Actions

Faced with the public indignation shown in the million-strong march, the government chose not to take action to de-escalate the situation. Quite the contrary, on the very evening of June 9th, Chief Executive Carrie Lam announced

that the amendments would go ahead as scheduled. The government's act, clearly against all common sense in public administration, left participants in great shock and anger.

Disillusion sparked even greater anger and resistance. On the 12th of June, the day the bill was scheduled for its second reading, huge crowds gathered in the Admiralty district, which houses the LegCo and government headquarters.

> I was out on the 9th of June. I had witnessed how the government ignored the opinion of all citizens.
>
> Ka-ming, university student

> On the 9th of June, seeing that a million had taken to the street, she (the Chief Executive) still stubbornly insisted on proceeding with the second reading. I can still remember how I felt at the time. It was like awaiting execution. It was like we were making our last cry before we were to die, and she still laid the knife on you.
>
> Zoe, civil servant

> In the evening (of the 9th of June), I reached the endpoint (of the march) .... It was totally crowded. There was a good vibe. Who would have thought that by 11 pm, we would hear the government [say] ... that the amendments would go ahead .... I thought: how can it be! ...it was not difficult to govern Hong Kong people – Hong Kong people have always been apathetic to politics .... If the government had said, "We have heard the public opinion and will postpone the matter ..., will do more consultation blah blah blah" .... then most people would have accepted the outcome .... Honestly, we were just looking for respect .... I was thereby motivated to participate time and time again.
>
> Steve, advertising worker

Protesters' disillusionment on the night of June 9th was to be surpassed by their even greater shock and dismay at the violent suppression of the protests three days later. On the 12th of June, police fired a massive amount of tear gas, cloth bags and rubber bullets at a peaceful rally, which was later defined by the police as riots.

Many citizens were trapped by police attack between the LegCo building and the areas around Citic Tower, where a peaceful rally had been approved by the police. The danger caused by the attack there far exceeded what the participants could have anticipated. University student Ka-ming was present. She recalled that at 3 pm that day, Legislator Claudia Mo (of the pro-democracy camp) announced that the mass actions had successfully led to the postponement of the LegCo meeting, but the bill was yet to be withdrawn. Ka-ming therefore decided to stay at Admiralty. As a result, she came to witness the disproportionate force the police used on the peaceful protest. Here she described the scene:

> All I could see was that [the protesters] moved one by one on to [the Admiralty Centre footbridge] .... My feeling was that they were bracing death because [they were] all injured. So such pain .... The police started their massive arrest and were madly, incessantly firing tear gas. This was the first time I experienced tear gas .... I went up the bridge again and was totally trapped .... Everyone was frightened. No one could see anything; the smoke was so bad .... All were crying. I even heard someone say, "Oh no, oh no! Am I going to die?" Because if we went down, we would run into the Raptors. Then we would be trapped again, not able to go down, not able to move, not able to breathe .... That was the first time when I felt I was near-death. Very angry! Since then, my friends and I were the same, [we] started to be very proactive, wanting to participate, wanting to do lots of things – but that came through a mental journey.

This shock and anger were commonly reported by our respondents, shared by even those who were not present that day.

> I felt rotten on June 12. I was watching the news all day and was aware of all that happened afterwards. I felt extremely shocked, deeply in pain. Cloth bags had already been fired then, which was very shocking to Hong Kong people. We also felt extremely angry.
>
> Zoe, not present on June 12

Marco was on the scene and witnessed how the police crack-down impacted the protesters' mental state:

> [The police] continued to fire tear gas. Many people didn't have goggles. I had brought some saline solution and was about to help a girl rinse out her eyes. She said, 'I'm not in tears because of the tear gas. I just don't understand why the police do this to us.' We were not armed in any way; it was such a peaceful march (rally)! ... [the protesters] were just singing, at most they threw water bottles, there were no iron bars or anything. I don't

understand why they had to fire tear gas. It was even more moderate than the umbrella [movement in 2014].

Marco, university student

Jim was helping at a supply stop at Admiralty alongside his friend. At first, he still considered himself an observer.

Up until 6–7 pm .... the atmosphere was still quite laid back. We didn't do anything violent. All of a sudden, riot police marched in from around the government headquarters and fired tear gas at us. I saw tear gas bombs landing right behind me. I had nothing except for a pair of goggles. My first reaction was to run .... I remember I cried. Not because of the tear gas, but because I could never have imagined that they would fire tear gas at me. My friend pulled me away. We went under a footbridge near the government headquarters. I was very lost, very helpless, very desperate. I think this was my beginning.

Jim, social worker

On the afternoon of the 15th of June, Carrie Lam announced a suspension to the amendments bill, but declared that it was only "to allow more time for communication, explanation, listening of opinions" and refused to take back the police characterization of what happened on the 12th of June as riots. Later that same day, 35-year-old Marco Leung Ling-kit climbed onto a platform at the Pacific Place shopping mall on Queensway to protest the bill and police violence on the 12th of June. He eventually fell to his death that night, causing a rapid escalation of the anti-extradition movement. The next day, the 16th of June, came the largest demonstration in the history of Hong Kong. The organiser, the Civil Human Rights Front, estimated the participation number at "two million plus one" – the one being Marco Leung Ling-kit.

Leung's death made an immense impact, and it seems young people were particularly affected. Three of our interviewees, two of them in their late teens and one in her early twenties, said his death consolidated their determination to continue participation in the movement:

6.15 [made me feel that as] there was a death involved, we could not let Carrie Lam get away with it.

Streambreaker, secondary school student

> The most unforgettable ... should be the most tear-inducing ... (June 16) was the march of the two million ... A *sau zuk*[2] has died. He was wearing [a] yellow [raincoat] .... [He] jumped. People went there (outside the Pacific Place). I began to move. Everyone was staying there. At that scene, people were all ... people were all very sad. We all blamed ourselves. Even though we didn't know each other, but this martyr (Leung), this *sau zuk* who had sacrificed himself, he used his life to ... to [support] this movement. Because of this event, my determination became firmer. Since then, things became unbearable for many people, they jumped to death .... It was terrible.
>
> Elf, shop assistant

> What I vividly remember is how Leung Ling-kit jumped off at Admiralty. I cried at home for a long time. It may be [when I] cried the fiercest during the whole movement.
>
> Wing, young female

The government's halting of the bill did not help to cool down the situation. In fact, the number of people who turned out at the next day's march doubled. Perhaps just as the respondents observed, Leung's death brought to the movement a sense of tragedy; nevertheless, the main driving force behind the protesters' participation was the government's stubbornness. As Steve said above, Hong Kong people were politically apathetic. Should the government have made the slightest gesture to demonstrate respect for public opinion, to consult the people, at least some would have "accepted the outcome". Unfortunately, as things developed, the course only ran in the opposite direction.

As the government refused to respond to the movement and as police repression escalated, the Anti-ELAB Movement quickly intensified in the following months. Police violence again and again exceeded people's worst expectations, with the most extreme instances being the 7.21 Incident[3] and the

---

2 Protesters call each other 'sau zuk', literally, 'hands and feet', originally a metaphor for siblings from the same parents. But in the Movement, it was used to allude to a comradeship in which people are committed to the same mission and feel part of each other.

3 Rumours circulated on the 21st of July that triad members would be attacking people in Yuen Long. That evening, an armed mob dressed in white showed up at Yuen Long MTR station and indiscriminately assaulted passengers and passers-by. Many called the police emergency hotline for help. It was not until more than half an hour later that the police finally arrived at the scene. For further references, see footnote 8, Chap 1 (Prelude).

8.31 Incident.[4] It can be seen from our interviews how these instances of police violence impacted on the participants, directly prompting them to reconsider their roles in the movement and leading the resistance onto a more radical path of no return.

---

4   On the evening of the 31st of August, a quarrel broke out between several anti-demonstrators and some protesters outside a train compartment at Prince Edward MTR station. Hammers were waved and fire-extinguishers were deployed as defense weapons, causing big clouds of discharge at the platform. Upon receiving reports, almost a hundred officers of the Special Tactical Squad and riot police arrived at the scene, rushed into a compartment, and started beating up passengers and releasing tear gas inside the compartments. Those assaulted by the police included children and at least one person in a wheelchair. The train was later moved into Yaumatei station, where many of those injured left on their own, and where police chased and expelled anyone present. The train compartments were left in total chaos. Journalists' photos show bloodied tissue paper, gauzes, diapers, etc. Prince Edward station was shut down by the police. Journalists and paramedics were refused entry; ambulances and the Fire Services' Mobile Command Unit were also rejected. The police later deployed a special train service to transport the injured to a different station, where the ambulances were finally allowed to collect and send the injured passengers to the hospitals. In the end, it took two and a half hours before the victims could reach the hospitals. As Prince Edward station and Mongkok station were shut down for a period of time by the police, who also refused to clarify what had happened inside the stations, including refusing to release CCTV footage, rumours started to spread that people had died inside the station from police assaults. The rumours continued to gain currency even when some injured passengers who were rumoured to have died appeared in public to clarify; so much so that for over a year, a shrine was set up outside Prince Edward station with citizens offering constant streams of flowers. For further references, see footnote 10, Chap 1 (Prelude).

CHAPTER 3

The Movement of No Return

For our interviewees, police brutality was the key factor behind the antagonism between government and the people, as well as the driving force for the Movement's escalation. The police brutality they themselves had suffered, or had witnessed, not only jolted their conceptions and feelings, but also drove them to reevaluate the nature of the government and the direction of the Movement, and to decide on their own commitment and role. Most participants showed that police brutality was the most common, most deeply felt, and significant experience of the Movement. Some of them were left with a sense of injustice and unfairness, others felt insult, anger, and incredulousness, yet others felt guilt (for other protesters' arrest and/or injuries) and hatred. However, none of them chose to retreat, but instead resolved to join the Movement with greater resolution, either taking up a supportive role, or even joining the frontlines.

The tragic and heroic moment of the Movement is that the participants joined it not because of hope and pursuit of realisable goals, but they were mainly driven by anger and a deep sense of injustice. "There are no rioters, there's only tyranny", and "Liberate Hong Kong, Revolution of Our Times" became the most popular slogans in the Movement, which emotionally mobilised more and more participants. While our respondents joined the Movement at different points, the motivation of their participation all shifted as the Movement unfolded: from "anti-amendment" to hoping to make the government responsive to the public, then protesting against the police's violent, unrestrained repression. In the following, we shall see how the change in motivation also brought along changes in the participants' roles. Respondents reported how their first-hand experience or witnessing of police brutality turned them from PRN (peaceful, rational and non-violent) protesters to 'valiant' protesters.[1]

After falling victim to police violence, Streambreaker, the secondary school student, experienced a profound sense of injustice and observed how his own mindset changed:

---

1 The Cantonese term "yung-mo" 勇武 was used to denote protesters who are in the frontlines, and who use more militant means. Here we use the word "valiant" for it, as an adjective or noun. Dapiran, in his book about the 2019 Movement, uses the word "braves" (Dapiran, 2020).

I would think that that day (the 7th of July) in Sheung Shui was when I turned from peaceful, rational and non-violence to valiant ... At first, I was just persuading the protesters to stay calm ... suddenly I saw that other people were beginning to charge, beginning to run .... I followed them. Halfway a chubby lad tripped and landed on my leg .... I struggled myself free from him and continued to run. I was caught up by some pepper spray at this time already. The riot police also hit my back with their riot shields. I had to keep running.

Fortunately, Streambreaker was not arrested this time. He was only hurt by the pepper spray. While being asked whether and why he became a Valiant, he patiently explained,

I was slammed by the police ... my eyes were sprayed. I felt that these actions were not necessary. ... I remember that when I was still a PRN, when I saw other people breaking bike chains, trying to tie the bikes to the crowd-control barriers, I would immediately stop them because those were private property. So intense was my moral feeling .... eventually I would keep quiet when I saw it happen again. ... But because of this experience (on the 7th of July), I decided to go (to all protests) whenever I could.

Likewise, university student Ka-ming felt injustice from her own frontline resistance. Adding to that, the arrest of her friend and the sacrifice of others all made her commit deeper to the Movement:

Chased by the dogs (police), first it was panic and fear, anger, and fury. Then I thought, why do you have to do this (to me)? Why? Truth be told that I am an ordinary person striving for what should be mine. Why do you have to treat me like this? Then later my friend was arrested, then even ... went on exile. Then came Chow Tsz-lok's death[2] .... I do not know

---

2   Chow Tsz-lok, a 22-year-old student from Hong Kong University of Science and Technology, died from falling from the third floor of a car park in Tsueng Kwan O, an area of anti-government protests on 8 November 2019. The protesters claimed that this accident had been caused by police's firing tear gas and use of brutal means to arrest them. See https://www.scmp.com/news/hong-kong/politics/article/3036833/hong-kong-student-who-suffe red-severe-brain-injury-after (last viewed 5 Sept 2022). The jury in the inquest delivered an open verdict as to the cause of his death. The coroner Ko Wai-hung said, on closing, that the inquiry was "almost close to the truth". He expressed hope that the truth could be revealed one day. See "Jury delivers open verdict on Chow Tze-lok's death", *The Standard*, 9 Jan 2021.

him personally, but I have friends who know him. He made me feel that the whole thing was very close to me. ... I felt that it was very absurd.

Cherry and her husband were professionally trained senior social workers. Nonetheless, after their first-hand experience of police violence, they were equally outraged:

> On my own mental journey, when I was hit by pepper spray on the 1st of July, this injustice done to me ignited an anger that was hard to quell. But I had to maintain my professionalism as a social worker, so I had no choice but to calm my own emotions first. But that truly had a huge impact [on me] .... I thought that the police were unforgivable .... Then this time, the [feeling of] injustice [done on me] by the "blue water" (tinted colour used by the water cannon to mark protesters) was even stronger .... My position (in the crowd) was not that of a 'chung chung ji' (a protester who is in advance of the demonstration) or a journalist. We were just a few people wandering around. Suddenly this water cannon truck came ... the blue water sprayed.

In fact, Cherry's husband, Tom, had already experienced the terror of unreasonable force applied by the police earlier on the 12th of June:

> Suddenly a loud noise came from around [the LegCo building]. We didn't recognise what it was. We thought something had fallen to the ground or (the protesters) started to tear things down. We didn't know what the cause was. Later, my eyes started to get very irritated, then we realised the first tear gas had been fired over there .... Luckily we were at the side of the carpark and could run away.

Seeing that the protesters on the side of Citic Tower were 'trapped in the cage', Cherry and her husband withdrew to near the Lennon Bridge.[3] Tear gas began to be fired also at the government headquarters. Cherry said,

---

https://www.thestandard.com.hk/breaking-news/section/4/162999/Jury-delivers-open-verd ict-on-Chow-Tsz-lok%27s-death (last viewed 5 Sept 2022).

3   During the Umbrella Movement in 2014, the sides of a stairway located in the Central Government Complex in Admiralty became a mosaic wall, with words and sketches on colourful post-it's stuck on it. This was called the "Lennon Wall", named after that in Prague which, prior to the downfall of the Communist regime, was a rare spot for expressions of irritation with the Czech government. Similar "Lennon Walls" appeared in various other locations in the city during the 2019 Anti-ELAB Movement. Like the Lennon Wall in Admiralty

Some shouted: 'Get on the bridge!'. Some had gone on to the platform and came back to say, 'There are Raptors up there!' ... The feeling was like – there was no way ahead, but soldiers were chasing behind .... I saw for myself how the riot police fired TG (tear gas) directly at the crowd. [The canisters] exploded right amidst the crowd, who had no time to escape. Many were crying .... That moment was – there were no words. I looked at the sky and thought: Do as you like, fire as you like; there is nothing we can do. Why don't you just open live fire?

The couple and another social worker colleague of theirs were again present in another rally on the 14th of July, which had been granted a "Letter of No Objection" from the police:

That incident in Shatin was devastating to me. What we saw (concerning the police manoeuvre) was no longer dispersing but rounding up ... The major fronts were at the swimming pool and Lucky Plaza. There was a "Letter of No Objection" for [the rally at the plaza in front of the town hall]. I started to tell other people to go back to [the plaza] when things started to go wrong. But even [the rally at the plaza] was suspended, people were ordered to leave by the police. It impacted me greatly because when we reached the exit of the carpark of Shatin Park, a team of Raptors suddenly came up. A group of people at the back had to retreat to [the plaza]. The press was not present there and my other colleagues were at those two fronts. Cherry and I, along with a female colleague, ran right into this group of Raptors. I went to ask them (the Raptors) to give the crowd more time to leave. A police officer put his baton on top of my head until another [riot police] dragged me away. It was only later that I realised I had scared my family, that it was a very dangerous moment.

Tom, social worker

Cherry recalled,

Another policeman was talking to me with his foot stepping on mine. The police were no longer here to protect us.

---

in 2014, these became major artworks of the Movement. The Lennon Wall in Admiralty is sometimes called the Lennon Bridge, because the staircase leads up to the footbridge crossing Harcourt Road.

Faced with these situations, Tom, as a social worker, had to suppress his own emotions to try to negotiate with the police and urge them to observe their code of conduct, e.g., tear gas must not be fired horizontally or targeted at the head, or when protesters were not charging, no guns should be fired nor even raised. Their effort would sometimes effectively calm the police down. But as police repression escalated, the line between what was lawful and what was unlawful became blurred. Even supporting and accompanying roles like those that Cherry and Tom took up became increasingly dangerous.

1   **The Tragic Night of 7.21 No Rioters without a Tyrannical Regime**

Cherry's sentiment that "the police were no longer here to protect us" was shared by many participants. As the police and the government failed in the roles expected of them by society, participants came to realise that the government was already corrupt and therefore the resistance should go further. The turning point was the 7.21 Incident, which occurred in the MTR (metro) station of Yuen Long. Like many others, Nan, a social worker, began his involvement in the Movement on the 9th of June. He described himself as a PRN and positioned himself as a supporter up until early July. On the 21st of July, he joined a march in Sheung Wan and helped set up a roadblock to stop the police from advancing. Later that night, he heard that the incident at Yuen Long was still on-going:

> And I learnt that some of our *sau zuks* ran into trouble when they were going home to Yuen Long. So [I] ended up going to Yuen Long too. (After midnight) [I] arrived in Yuen Long; from afar I could already see these men in white clothes. I saw for myself how their gear was more superior than any of ours. They were carrying steel rods, masks, and various weapons. But the police [acted as if] they didn't see them, standing with their backs to the white-clothed, facing the protesters. (The men in white clothes) obviously were carrying weapons but the police acted as if nothing happened. ...
>
> Who would have imagined that the police could allow these white-clothed men to do as they wished, carrying a range of weapons, and not perform their duty to protect the citizens? Their (the police's) attitude was arrogant, unreasonable. It felt so hopeless. I think this was why the violence escalated.

To many participants, the Hong Kong government would no longer listen to the people who rallied peacefully. It became difficult to change the situation using the previous method of peaceful appeals. Nan believed that the 7.21 Incident made a deep impact on the Movement and was a wake-up call to many, many Hongkongers, telling them that stronger resistance was required. Steve also observed how his wife's attitude changed since then. He said:

> My wife changed markedly after 7.21. Previously, she would tell me not to get too drawn into these things. After 7.21, we were uncontrollable .... Generally, we did some logistic work, formed human chains to transport supplies; we also purchased supplies from our own pockets.
>
> Steve, advertising worker

Like Nan and Steve's wife, many respondents mentioned the shock brought by the 7.21 Incident, the 8.31 Incident, and their first-hand experience on other occasions. They suddenly noticed that the behaviour of the police had shattered their previous understanding and expectations of the police, the government and even Hong Kong itself:

> A second incident happened in Yuen Long too on the night of 7.21 that I thought was outrageous. That was a very crucial watershed. In front of the camera, the police courted those people that we figured were triad members. (A police officer patted the shoulder of one of them.) ....
>
> Before this, perhaps [the public] knew that they were collaborating secretly, but this time, they were doing it explicitly; so even the most unaware were now awake .... After 7.21, PRN that I was, I also escalated: I started to wear black clothes, black trousers, wear a mask, cover my face; a hiking stick for self-protection. I began to buy spray paint to write graffiti. I knew that I wouldn't stand at the forefront, so I would also buy some laser pens to take some actions from a distance, [actions] that were not against the law. At a later stage, I felt I had to write graffiti, because I felt that fighting was only physical force while advocacy with words could last longer.
>
> Thomas, IT worker

The incidents in Sheung Wan and Yuen Long on the 21st of July ... I also went to Sheung Wan, whereas the incident in Yuen Long increased my acceptance of militant tactics. It was genuinely absurd and inconceivable:

the police leaving the scene, Ryan Lau[4] being beaten, protesters being beaten, Junius Ho[5] (seen congratulating members of the white-clad mob near the scene), etc. People couldn't accept that and were very angry that such a thing could happen.

Sunny, social worker

Many respondents were shocked by the 7.21 Incident, a trauma driving them to intensify their actions. The participants were furious that the government was not going after the police's abusive use of violence. To many, the 7.21 attack signified the collapse of Hong Kong's core values and institutions, going way below the bottom line of Hong Kong citizens. What's worse, the government was giving the triad gangsters in white-clothes a free hand; Elf, a shop assistant said, "it's like saying, 'That's okay you (the police) don't need to take any responsibility even if you beat someone to death.'" This itself was so provocative that anger reached a breaking point. This was a point of no return for Hong Kong.

2   To Resist by Any Means Necessary

Protesters felt that police brutality had become totally unrestrained. As they queried the legitimacy of the police and the government, they also began to consider whether their commitment to the resistance movement was appropriate and sufficient:

This government was not doing what the people wanted it to do, and it refused to correct itself. Should we still comply with it? That's why later I moved more and more to the forefront.

Raine, university student

---

4 Ryan Lau, former journalist and TV anchor, was involved in animal protection and environmental protection works. On the evening of the 21st of July, upon the mass attack in Yuen Long, he drove to the scene to help evacuate the victims. There, he was himself attacked by the 'white-cladded men'. With blood all over his face, he was sent to the hospital and required 11 stitches for his injuries. Based on his own memory and the accounts of over 40 eyewitnesses, he later published a Chinese book on the incident (Lau, 2020).

5 Junius Ho, an indigenous inhabitant of Tuen Mun in the New Territories, was elected legislator in 2016 and had been a controversial figure in the Establishment camp. On the night of the 21st of July 2019, a large gang of white-clothed men believed to be triad members attacked passers-by indiscriminately and fiercely with steel and rattan rods. Online footage showed Ho shaking hands with these white-clothed men, raising his thumb, praising them as 'hero' and taking pictures with them.

Streambreaker also did some serious politico-philosophical thinking of the political reality in Hong Kong:

> My thinking is that militant resistance [should only be done] when peaceful parades fail. The purpose of a peaceful parade is to awaken people's conscience. I listened to a philosophy program of the RTHK (the public broadcasting service in Hong Kong) which discussed whether violent resistance should be used. It mentioned that in a 'nearly-just society', when one exercises civil disobedience or adopts the 'love and peace' approach,[6] 'love and peace' is for awakening public conscience, and further to affect voting, and ultimately to achieve a certain outcome.[7] But under the Hong Kong system, we don't have 'dual universal suffrage' (universal suffrage for the Chief Executive and the Legislative Council); therefore, it would be ineffectual to use civil disobedience to awaken conscience and further to make influence .... We are not able to [change] the government in a peaceful or PRN way .... the Chief Executive would not listen .... Under such circumstances, [we] may need to resist 'by any means necessary' [as what Malcom X described].[8]

'Peaceful parades failed' in this case because of the governance fiasco that had originated in the lack of a democratic system. Many respondents echoed this view. For them, the most evident sign of governance breakdown was no doubt the deterioration and corruption of the police force. Zoe, the civil servant said,

---

6 This refers to the "Occupy Central with Love and Peace" campaign, a peaceful civil disobedience campaign first initiated in March 2013 by Rev Chu Yiu-ming, Prof Benny Tai and Prof Chan Kin-man. The campaign was eventually launched in September 2014 and became part of the Umbrella Movement (or Umbrella Revolution, as named by some) in October of that year.

7 *Rebellion is justified.* RTHK Talk Show – Philosophy Night 2018: https://m.facebook.com/rthktalkshow/posts/1945753955488736/ (no longer available).

8 Malcom X's notion of "by any means necessary" became very salient to reformers at his time. A leading figure of the American civil rights movement, Malcom X (1925–1965) is nevertheless controversial in his racial discourse and advocacy of violence. In a speech in 1965, he said, "We declare our right on this earth to be a man, to be a human being, to be respected as a human being, to be given the rights of a human being in this society, on this earth, in this day, which we intend to bring into existence by any means necessary." He contended that since the US government was not willing to and not capable of protecting the blacks, the blacks had to protect themselves. He founded OAAU (Organization of Afro-American Unity) and declared that with the organisation, he was determined to resist any invaders by any means necessary to fight for freedom, justice, and equality. See Malcom X, *By Any Means Necessary: Malcom X's Speeches and Writings*, New York, Pathfinder Press, 1992.

> [The police] have become an undisciplined force. They have power, they
> have arms in their hands .... The law enforcement is outrageous; there
> are not many more adjectives that can describe them. They use their
> own means, doing away with the court process. They take it in their own
> hands; they execute their own laws. This is something I don't think Hong
> Kong citizens can accept.

Strictly speaking, the police were not executing the laws of Hong Kong. Wan-
san, a graduate student also commented,

> The police are now a symbol of evil. If I were there at the scene, I would
> want to give them some punches too. When a police officer is beaten,
> you must ask why their image is so bad? ... Now everyone wants to beat
> the police. They have public power in their hands, but their image is
> so bad.

Beside the 7.21 Incident, the most memorable instance for Jason, a retail
worker, was the 31st of August on Harcourt Road. Tear gas and water cannons
were deployed at the bridge outside the People's Liberation Army Hong Kong
Building while Jason, with other people, were peacefully walking on the street.
He said,

> People were all just walking. All of a sudden, they (the police) fired the
> water cannon. ... it changed me. ... that made me feel that frontline sup-
> port was needed. Because many people had already been arrested at the
> time and many of the arrested were valiant *sau zuks*. ... We all began to
> feel that we should take a step forward, otherwise all frontline *sau zuks*
> will be arrested.

The filmmaker, Wang, was reflecting on institutional collapse in Hong Kong
when the trust in the police was entirely gone. He explained,

> When your trust in the whole society has collapsed, even something as
> simple as being robbed on the street, you will not be calling the police.
> [On the contrary,] I would have to fear that you will beat me up because
> I am wearing black clothes Why should I call the police? If someone
> stabbed me with a knife, I would only call the fire service because I don't
> want to call 999 (the emergency call number in Hong Kong).

FIGURE 2   Standing in protective gear. On August 20, 2019, a group of protesters in protective gear stood outside the Tuen Mun West Rail Station to make their appeal. On their placard were the words: "I'm just a timid wage earner. I wear my gear to work for fear of being suffocated by tear gas one day, of being chopped to death, of being shot in the eye by beanbag rounds; but the worst fear is the day when black and white are no longer distinguished."

Having experienced the escalations of the brutal suppression of the police in July and August, and the government not making any concession, most participants reached the conclusion that social governance had failed, and protest actions should escalate. The string of landmark events that ensued made our interviewees feel that not only individual citizens, but also the whole system was under assault. The non-response of the police in face of the indiscriminate beatings of passers-by by triad members on July 21st caused great anger and grief. The total inactivity of the police in this incident, and their failure to take up responsibility was totally unacceptable. Then on August 31st, the police attacked passengers ferociously in Prince Edward MTR station, and worse was yet to come. In November 2019, the police stormed the campus of the Chinese University of Hong Kong with countless volleys of pepper bullets and tear gas, as many people in the city viewed, via live broadcast, with anger and disbelief. Facing police brutality and government negligence, our interviewees saw systemic failure on three dimensions. First, normal social life was unhinged. Second, governance became ineffective, as the government connived with

FIGURE 3 Police fired tear gas. On November 11, 2019, many people responded to the call for a citywide strike in school, work and business by blocking the traffic from morning in various locations to stop work and business, hoping to force a response from the government and achieve the "Five Demands". Protests continued into the night. Here is a collection, assembled by some protesters, of the tear gas canisters fired by police that night outside the Tuen Mun West Rail Station. In the six months from June that year, police had fired more than 16,000 rounds of tear gas in total.

FIGURE 4 Fire arrows defend Chinese University. On November 13, 2019, after the defense battle for the Chinese University, protesters tested the firing of a DIY "fire arrow" around 2 am at No. 2 Bridge near Biotechnology Avenue by lighting an arrowhead wrapped with rags soaked in flammable liquids. However it was never put to use due to its short fire range.

FIGURE 5   Making petrol bombs. On November 13, 2019, after the defense battle for the
            Chinese University, a group of protesters were making petrol bombs around 6 am
            on Seaside Drive of the campus.

triad societies in assaulting innocent members of the public, thus giving police
a free hand in their callous repression and subverting public expectations and
losing its legitimacy. Third, peaceful protests seemed totally ineffective, as the
authorities turned a blind eye to all public demands expressed in an orderly
manner. This brought our interviewees to the realisation that the Movement
must escalate so that they could get closer to their goals.

CHAPTER 4

Be Water: Dying for the Political Demands

Remarkably, the radicalisation of the Movement did not lead to its splitting up. On the contrary, unprecedented tolerance and solidarity were consistently demonstrated. Protesters used slogans such as 'PRN and Valiants are one', 'Do not betray, Do not split'.[1] Respondents participated in the Movement with very clear motivations. At the beginning, they were motivated to stop the government from passing the amendment bill of the extradition law. Later, the 'Five Demands' emerged, as the regime continued to ignore the political aspirations of the million who went on the street and imposed disproportionate militant repression, classifying the peaceful rallies as 'riots'. Three of the 'Five Demands', raised at the two-million-strong march of June 16th, would become the focal points of the whole movement. They are, namely, withdrawal of the bill, retraction of the characterisation of protests as riots, and setting up of an independent commission of inquiry into police use of violence.

Withdrawal of the bill was indeed the starting point for the Anti-Extradition Bill Movement. The idea was to uphold the 'firewall' between Hong Kong and the political power of China. The demand for an independent commission of inquiry looked to re-establish both justice and the checks and balances on the police force through a mechanism familiar to the Hong Kong people. Unfortunately, one after another, incidents unimaginable until now unfolded: on the 14th of July, riot police fired pepper spray at crowds and rounded up protesters in the packed, Sunday shopping mall of Shatin New Town Plaza; on the 21st of July, triad gangsters beat up passers-by at Yuen Long MTR station without any police intervention; then the police themselves beat up citizens in MTR train compartments and barred paramedics and the fire service from entering the scene to save the injured on the 31st of August. For the respondents, these incidents marked the breakdown of the once-reliable social institutions and the betrayal of established social expectations, such as a government that was responsive to public opinion, a police force that was there to maintain social order, and – it goes without saying – a minimum level of social justice.

---

1   A study conducted in September 2019 found that participants generally had a high level of tolerance to radical tactics. See Lee et al. (2019), p. 18.

Aside from the Five Demands, many respondents also cited 'dual universal suffrage' (of the Legislative Council and the Chief Executive) as their goal. They contended that this right was granted to Hong Kong by the Basic Law (Jack, driver). They also believed that Hong Kong could only be safe when its government was mandated by the people. The city would then "have a protective shield" and not have to be subjected to the will of the Chinese communist regime (Lam, a salesperson). In addition, only under this basic condition can one of the five demands, namely, an independent commission of inquiry, the aspiration to restrain the police, be realised.

Many respondents expressed their loss of confidence in the SAR government. They found that for years, the government had only been paying lip service to the deep-seated issues of Hong Kong. Lacking governing capacity, it had long neglected the welfare agenda, e.g., education, housing, and health system. Its capacity to govern had sunk so low that even in managing emergencies, it was outperformed by Shenzhen and Guangzhou. Jack, a driver, said,

> The two super typhoons, Hato [in 2017] and Mangkhut [in 2018], especially the Super Typhoon Mangkhut, brought Hong Kong into chaos for most of the day. [On the day of] Typhoon Hato ... there were over 700 reports of fallen trees .... In comparison, Guangzhou and Shenzhen had already suspended work, suspended school, suspended all commercial activities and production, all four of these. Why didn't [the Hong Kong government] follow suit? ... Bread-and-butter issues are constant concerns. It's clear that [the government] doesn't even have common sense. Cash handouts will most please Hong Kong people, but [the government] can't even do it [right] .... It took them so much time just to make a cash handout of HK$4,000.

What kind of an institution do the respondents seek then? Simply speaking, they aspire to a government that is accountable to the public; therefore, a robust rule of law is a requisite. Only with this requisite can government power be checked and balanced, and justice, freedom and even welfare issues guaranteed. Amy, a senior engineer, commented,

> Rule of law and justice are more than just the existence of the law. They depend also on ... a government that observes that law, a police force that does not beat people up; and, even if a police officer committed an offence, he would be duly punished. But as we can see now, those with power can do whatever they like (with absolute power). [If] the powerless are doing the right thing and [those in power] can say [the powerless] are

wrong, that would be very problematic. If justice ceases to exist, or worse still, it is the government that leads the annihilation of justice, then this place is in deep trouble.

Susanne, an educator, further explained,

> [People] stand up to resist because [they] want to establish a relatively good system; they don't want things to go backward. But think about it: in recent years, the ICAC (Independent Commission Against Corruption) has been effectively garbage, no? ... The government is giving people the impression that it has become so corrupt that it doesn't even care to pretend.

Susanne was angry that, starting from the beginning, the movement was only about the fugitives' law, but due to violent police repression which, in turn, was condoned by the government, the protesters had no choice but to attack the whole system. She said,

> It was about the political regime. People's freedom has been slowly eroded; the rule of law has been eroded. ... Their (police's) lawless behaviour itself is an assault to the rule of law, isn't it?

Sheung, who was working at a law firm, was even more furious than Susanne, and she expounded,

> The police don't need to bear any consequences for breaking the law. This is already an assault to the rule of law. And the Chief Executive was still thanking the police! [2] How can a regime talk about rule of law when it stands by a lawless police force? [The government] is constantly talking about rioters undermining the rule of law. The truth is that it is the government itself [who is undermining it] .... [Under these circumstances,] the core values of Hong Kong are eroded.

---

2 On the 8th and the 9th of August 2019, Carrie Lam, the Chief Executive, visited and met police officers at the Central Government Offices, various regional police headquarters and stations, and a disciplined services quarter, during which time she thanked the police force and pledged to fully support their work. See 'CE thanks the Force for its contribution', *Offbeat: the newspaper of the Hong Kong Police Force*, 1142, August 28 to September 10, 2019. https://www.police.gov.hk/offbeat/1142/eng/index.html (last viewed 7 Sept 2022).

As seen above, the respondents gradually developed a clear social and political vision. This vision involves a government that observes the rule of law, demonstrates justice and accepts public check-and-balance. Therefore, the respondents' goal rests in the so-called 'Dual Universal Suffrage' – universal suffrage for the Chief Executive and the Legislative Council, a right that most respondents pointed out is granted by the Basic Law. As highlighted at the beginning of this study, the Movement, by this point, had rapidly evolved and expanded from a movement of a single agenda about the fugitives' bill to become a general movement for democratic reform.

1   "No Central Stage": Each Finds His or Her Own Role in the Movement

Without a central organisation leading the movement, one main characteristic of the 2019 Anti-Extradition Bill Amendment Movement was that participants initiated their own actions which were mostly complementary to each other, as described in the Movement's catchphrases: "No central stage", "Brothers (and sisters) climb a mountain, everyone makes one's own effort". In their empirical research, scholar Francis L.F. Lee and his team concluded that when a strong resistant organisation or party politics was lacking, "self-mobilisation" had become the characteristic of the Hong Kong local resistance movement. Furthermore, taking the lesson from the failure of the 2014 Umbrella Movement, the 2019 resistance movement had promoted "no central stage" and "be water" since its beginning. On the one hand, this reduced the pressure to reach consensus on the movement's guiding ideology and strategies. On the other hand, it also removed the burden of stationing in and defending a "battleground" (Lee et al., 2019, p. 15).

Similarly, although we have discussed the respondents' various roles in the Preface, these roles are far from reflecting the multifaceted and ever-changing circumstances of their participation. In the following, we will describe the respondents' considerations in choosing the role(s) they took up and how they made the decision without centralised coordination. Wang, the filmmaker, illustrated this quite well:

> On June 12, I initially didn't realise that the riot police were so close to the pot[3] (in front of the Legislative Council). They started to fire tear gas.

---

3   The "pot" is a nickname for the sheltered protest area in front of the Legislative Council complex, which is shaped like a pot.

I looked across in front of me, (and thought) 'oh my, big trouble!' A group of people dashed through the revolving door in the Citic Centre. This would lead to people tripping and stepping on each other .... I walked calmly ... Back on the road, I didn't get stepped on at all ... Everyone was moving in an orderly fashion. That sense of looking out for each other, as if we all knew why we came out.

This phrase, "as if we all knew why we came out", speaks of the common goal all participants recognised and shared without saying it. It was this goal that functioned to coordinate and consolidate the Movement. Acting like a choir, participants consciously played different parts and took up different positions as a team, albeit without centralised coordination.

2   Be Water: Ever-Changing Positions

In fact, most participants did not stay in the same positions. Rather, they moved back and forth between the front and rear support. With the evolving situations and what they encountered in the Movement, where they positioned themselves changed. Loafer, a university student, changed his role after being arrested. He had begun to participate in the Anti-ELAB Movement on June 9th. He stood closer and closer to the front over the many subsequent times he went out. Participating in the July 27th "Liberate Yuen Long" event, he saw the Raptors (Special Tactical Contingent) beating people up, leaving behind a pool of blood on the ground. Loafer said, "Indeed (we) have seen this a lot in movies. But when I saw it in person, it was shocking."

Soon afterwards Loafer was arrested by the Raptors. He told us, "[I] was beaten up all over my head and shoulders," taken to the hospital and then the police station. After the arrest, he felt "a bit exhausted and wanted to rest a bit but would still go out to join actions such as human chain and other PRN (peaceful, rational, non-violent) activities, so as to add one more headcount ...." He continued to say, "sometimes, it was also helpful to act as a 'lookout guard' on the internet to report news. Sometimes [I] would also share with others what to pay attention to upon arrest, [including the time] when a friend's friend got arrested and my friend called to ask me what to do."

It is not uncommon to hear the "evolutionary" story of participants from being PRN (peaceful, rational, non-violent) to being a "Valiant" in the Movement. According to Elf's observation, "Many [people] have begun to take up initiative to help. We are progressing. (Ask: Some people in the rear didn't want to move to the front. Guess they didn't feel they had the ability?) Yes ...

some would assist the rally in the rear, to help keep up the head count .... Not just standing there daydreaming, but really looking around to see how to help, such as when we set up roadblocks, many people in the rear would help take apart fences, open up umbrellas (to make sure the faces of frontliners would not be caught by cameras, or to shield off tear gas canisters) and collect things for roadblocks to prevent [the riot police] to push forward, or at least, to slow them down."

The development of the situation was such that protesters had no other way but to respond according to changing circumstances or move further to the front due to increasing police suppression. Oliver, a secondary school student, said,

> The first time I was in the front line (on June 12th), I was part of the supplies chain in Pacific Place .... bringing with me a helmet, N95 (mask), a safety goggle, just a simple 3M goggle, wrapped in cling wrap. What they (the police) did from June 9th to late July had become so unacceptable to anyone that it had gone below the bottom line. ... That's why, (people) rebelled, moving further to the front, more and more to the front.

Reviewing the "evolution" process she and her friend(s) had gone through, Ka-ming, a university student, had a similar reflection:

> Did we wear full gear every time we went out? No. We didn't have this concept at the beginning. It was really a slow process of pushing more and more toward the front. I met a group of like-minded people who told me what I needed to do and helped me buy the gear .... (A friend) happened to pass by (where the August 31st Incident happened). But after experiencing events like that, he also came out more. We're similar in this regard .... The whole situation is so bad. But I feel what is good is how much Hongkongers have evolved to be where we are. (I) see how people have evolved one step at a time. After that incident, this friend learnt first aid and took the qualification test. I know quite a few people like that .... On June 9th, I was PRN (peaceful, rational, non-violent), and later got pushed to (become) so daring as to enter the Poly (Polytechnic University of Hong Kong – referring to the siege in November that year) .... In fact, I struggled a lot. I am actually a very timid girl .... I often say no one was born knowing how to resist and revolt. We are all growing.

Since June 2019, the Movement had grown more and more intense. This was surely an interactive dynamic resulting from the government and police's

iron-fist policy. Different participants had different reactions during this process. Lala was a dental assistant. Her participation process was perhaps quite
typical:

> Slowly I felt my hatred level rise .... I also ... struggled a lot when the
> hatred level gradually increased .... The first incident when someone got
> shot in the eye[4] .... Wow! The Hong Kong Police could behave like that ...
> (I) felt so shocked and realised that nothing could .... (Ask: Stop (them)?)
> Yes. (Then) more dead bodies (were found) in the sea, human life .... One
> time when things were starting, I (didn't) protect myself very well. I put
> down my anti-gas mask on the side, I was already picking up bricks. In
> the beginning I would be watching them take things apart and throw
> things. I had never picked up offensive weapons. But (that time) I began
> to pick up what's around, pick up tools .... (Ask: to protect yourself?) ....
> No. (I) was really planning to fight with them, that is, to attack. The bricks
> were intentionally sharpened. (A young person reminded her to wear
> the anti-gas mask at this time) .... In the meantime, (I) thought .... I was
> in such rage that others could also feel it .... (I) didn't have this before.
> Although I would watch and carry an umbrella to help, do small things,
> such as pushing cars, I had never thought of attacking others.

Like Lala, Raine, a university student, was another young female person who
moved further and further to the front. In early June she distributed publicity
materials in districts she felt familiar with. One time when she was yelled at
as "garbage" by an 'auntie' (a middle-aged woman), she got nervous and cried.
But she "would not cry anymore when encountering the same situation later".
On June 11th, she went with a group of 8 to 10 friends to the area near the
Legislative Council building. "Staying overnight .... that day was the first time
I got the 'stationery' they distributed, that is, self-protection gear. (My friends)
had experience participating in social movements. But that was my first time,
until the next morning on the 12th, around 11 am and 12 pm, we were in the
middle position at that time, helping to pass on supplies .... Later I moved
more and more to the front."

---

4   On 11 August 2019, a young woman had her right eye injured during a clash between the pro-
    testers and the police, claiming that it was injured by police's bean-bag bullets, but had never
    reported to the police. Later the police obtained her medical report with a court warrant
    that had not been presented to her. The young woman applied for judicial review but lost.
    Regardless of what the truth was, this incident was one of the trigger points in the Anti-ELAB
    Movement. See footnote 2, in Chap 1 (Prelude).

FIGURE 6   Standing in silent protest. On August 12, 2019, protesters demonstrated at the
airport by standing in silence to protest against an incident the day before in
which a female voluntary first-aider in Tsim Sha Tsui was allegedly hit in her right
eye by a bean bag round fired by the police.

Raine explained why she moved more and more to the front, "This government isn't doing what the citizens want them to do. It is unwilling to right the wrong. Should we still comply with it?" Often, she would stand in the front row with an umbrella on the scene during the clash, relying on the map and information posted on social media about where the police were located. "I gave up staying in the frontline later because I felt the information I received was not adequate to help me assess whether I should charge. I was afraid that I might get others into trouble if I made a wrong assessment."

Although Raine did not stay in the frontline, she was nevertheless arrested in October. She was on bail at the time of the interview and would not go out for the time being. She said, "If I was arrested again, (I) would immediately be brought to a court hearing. There would be one person less in the future movement. But if I bear with it now, there will be one more person (in the movement)." She then hoped to collate the numbers of people who were arrested and wounded and even the information of those who had died because of the movement. She explained, "Perhaps finding out why they were arrested, though

I know it would be difficult to find people who were willing to come out. I felt I could compare the average number of deaths before and now, like working on an individual assignment, an IES (independent enquiry study, which was part of the 'Liberal Studies' subject in secondary school). This would allow people in future to judge the right and wrong of this movement."

Many respondents talked about their "moving more and more to the front". When they were on the scene, different participants would choose different positions in accordance with their expertise. For example, Wang, the film-maker, began to participate in the Movement and marched on June 9th. He described himself as timid but could find his role based on his loud voice. "Because I have a loud voice, people can hear me when I shout on the spot. (I would shout) 'Don't run! Don't run! (We) would step on people causing death! Don't run!' And we would also let's count one, two, one, two, count faster. There are many people behind. Walk a bit faster!' That is, to convince people to leave. 'Stand further apart!' You can feel that this is useful. You could see the crowd loosen up a bit. You see that when people heard someone call out, (their mind) got a bit settled. You would feel that you were useful."

As regard to aggressive action, Wang would consider the following in deciding whether to do it or not:

> Many times, I saw (people) passing bricks. When it came to my hand, I really couldn't do it. I was afraid to hurt others, afraid of legal conse-quences ... I threw it (the brick) away .... To be honest, I felt cowardly. But how can we justify ourselves to shoot? That is, can you point at the enemy side and shoot? .... Even if the bullet doesn't hit anyone, you have the intention to shoot .... It is a psychological threshold. So, I would put the brick down. Then a 'pop' sound, someone next to me fell. I would pick her/him up and leave.

Jim was a social worker. Compared to his peers in social work, he would not go to the front row at the scene. "One day, I happened to meet a female friend in social work. She wore the social worker identity card. She was very brave, wearing a helmet, an anti-gas mask, and nothing else. I asked her afterwards why she would stand tall (in the first row) and not be afraid they (the police) would really shoot. She said, 'It would be good if they shoot me. This would create some noise. I am taking care of the vulnerable groups and condemning what the police did wrong.' She wanted to have this effect. I have to say I don't have this courage. Therefore, I focused my duty on putting out fire and taking care of supplies."

Susanne was another young social worker. She felt that the "Battlefield social work"[5] peers were very brave. On the first Saturday of July, she began to realise that she could participate in the Lennon Wall work. She said,

> (I) would stay for a long time, like from 9 pm to 1 am. While reading the memos, I met groups of 'kaifongs' (residents in the neighbourhood) of all professions and occupations: medical health workers, secondary school teachers .... We took up different roles. They were more ahead of me .... Some elderly people objected. But there were also students and 'kaifongs' (who participated). With lots of conflicts every day, there was much need to defend our spot. Everyone took turn to guard (the Lennon Wall) for 7–8 hours .... There were only 10 people in the beginning because most had to work. Therefore, there was usually no one in the morning, until 4 pm when secondary school teachers got off work, as well as students. I would arrive at 6 pm. (I) also collected supplies, purchased pens, memos, snacks, etc. It was a very lovely place .... When (I) studied social work, (I) knew 'kaifong' (community) work was very difficult, very abstract; now I was experiencing it in reality .... Therefore, although I am a social worker, I think one can do more outside of the social work role.

Another social worker, Winnie, had gone to protest sites on different days, had been a "weather forecaster" (collecting and distributing information about where the police were, online), had helped open umbrellas to shelter the "fire magicians", had also helped to douse tear gas canisters and support the arrested, looked for escape routes for the protesters who were trapped, etc. In one of the marches, she also helped with voter registration (for the upcoming Legislative Council election in September 2020). "I was thinking what else could be done other than marching? ... Some people set up a street booth to help voter registration. I also thought since a Legislative Council still exists in Hong Kong, we could do more in this position. We chose a location beside a mailbox. The completed forms were immediately put in the mailbox after the registrants filled it out. We finished 6000 forms that day. The mailbox was completely full. We then went to another mailbox to set up a booth and continued."

Whether it was in the frontlines or simply staying on the scene, participants each found their own position to contribute to the Movement. To everyone, contributing itself was a practice as well as the construction of an important

---

5   "Battlefield social work" began in June 2019, comprising volunteer social workers who provided humanitarian aid on the scene during the protests as well as support to those who were arrested or charged.

value. In the words of Lam, a salesperson who was concerned about state surveillance on society, "Do whatever (you) can do .... Ask oneself what one can do. One must find one's own value, not (wait for) others to tell you what to do." Or, as the dental assistant Lala said, "The greatest impact this Movement has on me is a sense of responsibility. I keep saying to my younger brother and myself, 'Don't think that you can't do anything. Everyone has the capacity to fulfil one's responsibility. You fulfil your own responsibility and do not mind too much what you (can) do.' That's what I told myself every night."

Similarly, what was most important to most of the participants was to have no regret in their life. Kiki, a secondary student said, "(I) have not thought about whether (we) would win. (I) just feel if I don't come out now, when I get asked by the next generation several decades later what I have done for Hong Kong, I would have to reply: 'nothing but just sat there'. I don't want to give such an answer to the next generation." Perhaps this sense of responsibility among the participants was the driving force of this highly self-mobilised social movement. When there was "no central stage" and when everyone was in the "be water" state, a shared tacit understanding with a sense of direction was maintained.

FIGURE 7   Dousing a tear gas canister. On October 21, 2019, after a rally outside the Yuen Long West Rail Station to commemorate the July 21st Incident, demonstrators dispersed to the Yuen Long town centre, where they blocked roads in protest. A passer-by outside Yuen Long Plaza doused a tear gas canister fired by the police.

CHAPTER 5

Radiating the Movement: Multiple Roles of Backup Support

Given the numerous participants and intense activities in the Anti-ELAB Movement, one would assume that there was a complex coordination and even organisation behind it. However, almost none of our participants belonged to any organisation or even group, but instead, they were self-motivated and self-directed in their choice of tasks and roles in the Movement, or in individual episodes. Two major characteristics came out from their experience. First, every person found a position suitable for him/herself, and in a situation where no one was in charge, a self-emerging coordination "naturally" evolved in the process. Second, the position and form of participation of our interviewees changed in response to external circumstances and their personal situation. Yet, none of them had given up.

Generally, our interviewees made their choice of positions or roles in the Movement according to their own abilities, expertise, personal concerns or even worries, as well as the needs arising on the spot. Middle-aged or older persons, being less physically fit than younger ones, and having heavier family responsibilities, usually took up backup or support work. These included: support work on the spot, e.g., providing first aid, inventory transport, message transmission (so-called "sentinel" work), offering transport for retreating protesters, recording happenings on the spot, accompanying and supporting youngsters on the spot, sheltering protesters with umbrellas, or trying to mediate between the police and protesters. Outside the streets, backup or support work also came in various forms, including disseminating information over social media, making publicity materials to galvanise support, drawing maps to inform frontline protesters about ways of escape, as well as gathering donations and mobilising other necessary support resources.

Our interviewees would also adjust their roles or positions according to changes in the circumstances and their personal situation. There were protesters who, after having been arrested, backed away and restricted themselves to peaceful protests or even stayed away from street protests altogether to avoid being arrested again while on bail. Some of them might take up backup positions away from the streets, like passing messages and information on the internet ('*tin man toi*', meaning "observatory"), analysing the situation ('*laang hei gwan si*', literally meaning military adviser in an air-conditioned room), or providing counselling to those who had been arrested.

Some interviewees would take up multiple roles either at different stages of a protest action, or on different fronts in the Movement. They might, for example, buy and transport supplies, offer free rides, make international contacts, build up support networks, do publicity work and so on. In their eyes, no matter whether they were on the frontlines, doing backup work on the spot or elsewhere, they were all choosing their own positions to contribute to the Movement. Here we not only see choice and self-direction, but also responsibility and sacrifice.

Elf was a shop assistant. He quitted his job to fully participate in the Movement after he got more and more involved. He described his multiple roles as follows:

> I am a PRN (peaceful, rational, non-violent), mainly to help with supplies .... In fact, I have been a 'parent' (volunteer driver picking up young people from protest sites) too. I would stay behind to be a 'parent' after a rally has ended, and help with supplies again afterwards, then also be a rear guard, and later go to the front to set up roadblocks. I would take up whatever position is needed .... Currently, I have been doing less with supplies ...., rather, (I) run to the front to help set up roadblocks and be 'fire magician' (to light up fire) .... After I've picked up the children (young protesters), it's often already past 6 am by the time I get home. Sometimes there would be a meeting at 3 am. (I) would not get to sleep until after the meeting .... Many 'parents' stay behind until the very latest because (we) don't know if there are any 'abandoned kids'.

1   We Provide Supplies to Save Our Children

Backup support provided by the participants radiated the Movement, touching people from different ranks to support it. Some participants knew early on that their role would be backup support for the young people who were in the forefront of the Movement. These participants were mostly older, such as 30 or 40 years old who were aware that they were physically less mobile than the younger people, or because they had their own small children or parents to take care of.

Wing was a young female participant in the Movement who had to look after her mother. She went to the front on June 9th and 12th, standing in the first few rows facing the riot police. But since her mother joined her at the rallies after June 16th, she dared not stand too close to the frontlines. "Because (I) was with my mother, (I) later took up many other different roles .... such as purchasing and distributing supplies, being part of the supplies team, and then doing various publicity activities and sharing them on social media, then helping with the Lennon Wall .... And later I tried to help take care of those young people who were arrested."

Henry, a clerical staff, was not optimistic about the Movement from the beginning. He participated only to protect young people as much as possible and to reduce the injuries that might be inflicted on them.

> Because (I) can't be in the frontline, nor can (I) produce beautiful publicity materials, (laugh) (I) can only do some peripheral and trivial supportive tasks .... I don't have children ... My parents are still healthy ... (I) don't have a great (financial) burden. (I) can say that my 'to-be-sacrificed score' is high.

On June 12th, Henry initially helped in the first aid station in front of the Legislative Council. Later when the police used pepper spray and fired tear gas at a short distance, he helped move the supplies to the legitimate meeting place, that is, at the entrance of the Citic Centre. As there was too much tear gas and there was no place to turn back to, people could only retreat into the building. Because he was accompanying a young person who had broken his leg, together with a medical aide, Henry was forced to stay inside the building which was filled with heavy smoke from the incessant tear gas fired at the retreating protesters. It was then that he witnessed a horrific scene of mass casualties that might have happened had the people panicked. Luckily, the collective calm among the protesters saved them from this fate.

One month later, Henry heard that a large group of triad society members were planning to attack and injure people in Yuen Long. He was a resident in Yuen Long and was familiar with the area. He went to Yuen Long MTR Station early in the evening of July 21st to observe the nearby area, thinking that he could immediately send out messages through social media if he noticed any danger. Until around 10:30 at night, he saw that nothing had happened and so he was about to take the metro home. As soon as he stepped into the metro station, however, he saw two men in white T-shirts each holding a stick and chasing after a young man. Henry ran forward to try to stop them. The stick had already hit the young man. A section broke off and flew over, hitting Henry's foot which bled immediately and got swollen. Bearing with the pain, he went to the mall's customer service for first aid supplies and sat on the floor guarding the broken stick as a piece of evidence at the crime scene.

Eventually, to avoid his own injury worsening, Henry went to the second floor and entered a packed metro train compartment to go home. How could he have imagined the 10-minute horror that followed? Henry saw firsthand how the white-shirt gangsters tried charging into the compartment and assaulting people, "just like what was seen on television (later that evening)". An elderly woman and a young woman were terrified, as they crouched next to him. Near the door were several young people and an elderly man whose head was bleeding from the attack. The railway coach did not move. People near the door pleaded with the white-shirt people not to attack any more. Henry did not forget his duty to collect evidence and kept his phone on to video-record. After 40 minutes, the coach finally moved. Passengers who did not know each other discussed how to escort the elderly man for medical care. Henry took the responsibility to escort the elderly woman to go home by taxi. He did not dare post his video recording on Facebook. Instead, he sent it to his friends and asked them to forward it to the media.

Like Henry, many adults wanted to help the young protesters. Wendy, an accountant, told us that her role was "in the middle towards the frontline, that is, opening the umbrella to screen off the police, and transporting supplies such as clothes (for protesters to change), first aid supplies, etc .... When they said water cannons would be used, people needed to retreat. We would not need to follow the main group and leave immediately. We would run to some branch-off location to be a sentinel again, that is, to look around and see how the situation on the street was, read the social media ... report the situation to social media groups, provide them with information about routes they could take to go home .... I would not give up on the young people. If we are afraid even with the gear we are wearing, how much more fearful would they (young people) be? In fact, they didn't have anything .... They were fighting for what they wanted. How should I say this? To a certain extent I am grateful to them .... I am just coming out to help them. I am not as selfless as they are to give up their future to fight for our freedom and democracy."

Mei and Yat-nim were a couple, having two children of elementary school age. They explained why they tried the best to participate in providing backup support after June 12th.

> (On June 12) there were a group of young people in the front. Those in the first row shouted, '(we) need people!'. A large group of people behind me immediately surged to the front, without hesitation. I was so close to the Legislative Council Building at that time. If I just took one step forward, I would be on that street. (But) I just stopped and stood there, thinking about all the 'baggage' I was carrying, could I step forward? Even though

it was not so serious at the time, I was still a bit afraid. But the young people were all pushing through to the front without looking back. At that moment (I was) one of those so-called 'useless middle-aged', or you feel useless. You can only transport supplies. You are very sad and yet also feel moved.

Because (we) have children, when you look at those young people, if they were your children, how would you feel (watching them being beaten up like that by the police)? (You) would feel sad, wouldn't you?

Initially positioning himself as a supporter only, the young traditional Chinese medicine practitioner, Terry, participated in the marches and rallies in June and July but was never at the forefront. He was then away from Hong Kong briefly. Upon returning to the city in the second half of July, he saw that:

(The situation) had become entirely different. Many people were injured. Many were beaten by the police, injured by tear gas ... once I had seen these, I went to every single event after I returned to Hong Kong. I felt that since I knew Chinese medicine, there must be some ways I could help people.

During this time, Terry provided voluntary treatment to those injured in the resistance. "Some of those wounded had their entire back in bruises. Some were from beating, some from slamming, some were hit by rubber bullets. The bruises could be really deep. [At the sight of these,] I would ask: how can [people] do such a thing to a human being?"

Aside from voluntary treatment, Terry would also find time to go to protest sites to help buy and sort supplies, and to stand as 'sentinel', etc. Sometimes he would witness riot police kneeling on protesters' necks to hold them to the ground. Then he would try to shout to the police that necks must not be compressed. But when more riot police came to take the arrestees into police vans, he could do nothing further and would feel very guilty about it. These frontline experiences made him an even more committed participant of the resistance movement.

2   We Are Drivers Covering the Young People to Leave the Scene

Other adults who had a car most often acted as "school bus" drivers, that is, volunteering to pick up young people in the frontline and drive them away from the scene. Kei, an IT programmer, had a car which made it convenient for him to deliver supplies and pick up protesters. "I am a (freelance) IT worker and I have a car. I would use my advantage to assist the movement within my (physical) limitation, (mainly) to deliver supplies." Bat, an administrative personnel officer who owned a car, also used it to pick up protesters. He said,

> Often at the end of the rally or when tear gas was fired, I would go back to my car and wait for the right opportunity to pick up people on the scene to leave .... I often told my friends and even my girlfriend, 'I am a disperser.' I wanted everyone to go home safe.

Jack was indeed a professional driver who would spend a few hours a day picking up young protesters and giving them some protection. Looking physically like a policeman, he had to ask help from his female friends to go with him:

> I saw some 15–16 years old teenagers one evening. They were wearing tear gas masks. I drove them home .... I rarely asked people anything, very sensitive. Some people thought that I looked like a policeman (due to my physical build). One person asked me if I were a 'dog' (police) .... Therefore, I often went out with a female friend.

Sesame, an educator, formed a driving team rotating to pick up young participants at different places. He said, "A friend called me one evening after June 12th. He works as a driver in goods delivery. We are very close friends. We have been playmates together since childhood and we played ball games together since our time in secondary school. He said, 'Hey, I have a car. Let's work together!' Of course, we both have our own families. We couldn't go to the frontlines. But we could do what we could within our capacity. That's how we started to work as a team. Other friends joined us afterwards. We were mainly volunteer 'school bus' drivers."

Victor was a music teacher. He began to participate on-site in early June. Watching the authority's increased use of violence (he specifically mentioned the July 21st Incident) had transformed his views and made him participate more in backup support by connecting with his students:

> I was afraid at the beginning ...but I began to change slowly. Watching so many people offering themselves (to the Movement), and the young people who were even willing to sacrifice themselves, (I) felt I couldn't back down .... Later I thought about volunteering to pick up and drive people away from the scene. Therefore, I was mainly a volunteer driver in August and afterwards .... I connected with my students who produced publicity

materials and shared different information with each other, link(ing) up a network .... As well, they also hoped to drive and pick up *sau zuks*. So, I put them in touch with a student who was responsible for arranging car teams. Parishioners in my church also helped with driving. I think many people wanted to participate in backup support.

3   Using Social Media for Advocating: We Are People's Reporters

Other than volunteer drivers, different participants would also take up distinctive positions according to their abilities and skills and the needs of the Movement. One of the prominent roles is using social media channels extensively to voice their opinions, advocate their concerns and actions, and influence people of other political camps. For instance, other than being "sentinels", Mei and Yat-nim also found another role: "We had another role, that is to take more photos and videos so that others would know what really happened on the scene ... whether as a people's reporter, or as a record for ourselves, to remember what happened in this city at the time. We even shared all our photos and experience with our children .... as well as posted them on social media platforms. We didn't mind people knowing we had gone (to the scene)."

King Carp, a secondary school student, secretly bought and delivered supplies to protest sites with her schoolmates, without letting her parents know. But by mid-August she only dared to go to rallies and marches that had received the police's Letter of No Objection. Upon increased police suppression in late August, she only dared to stay home and work with her 13-year-old younger sister as "air-conditioned advisers" (people who were removed from the ground in giving their opinion or advice). That involved watching the protest livestreams and posting information about police manoeuvres and action on social media. "We had two phones, plus an iPad. We pretended to study (at home), but we were actually watching livestreams of events. We watched different streams and retweeted, looking for where a blue flag (police warning signal that they would take action to disperse an illegal assembly) was raised. Because there are 18 districts, many friends went to different places. They asked me to help. 'Blue flag in Shatin', 'Be careful in Wong Tai Sin. (Tear gas) may be fired.' I know this kind of 'air-conditioned advisers' are denigrated in some (social media) posts .... But one cannot do without (this kind of people like us). Every role is important."

Andy was a private tutor. Because she had a weak respiratory system, she dared not go to the protest sites. Graduated from journalism, she cared a lot about message transfer. She would stay home to forward messages. "In addition to forwarding messages on social media, (I) would also send out more neutral and certainly correct texts to guide others' thinking. I believe this is a way of peer influencing. I didn't go out but stayed home most of the time. (I) would assess whether the messages were true or false. Some messages were negative. Even if they were true, I would not forward (them) .... It was more effective to discuss with people who held different political views. Even though there might be different political views, people could still find an alignment ... for example, 'we all like peace' .... Based on this point to start a conversation, bit by bit, (then) extending it further and raising questions for their reflection."

Lam was a salesperson. She was particularly concerned about state surveillance. She set up a social media group with friends to send out specific information about AI (artificial intelligence) lamp poles, AI facial recognition systems, the social credit system and metadata surveillance. They also printed flyers on how to avoid surveillance and distributed them in crowded areas to remind people how to protect themselves and avoid being charged by the authorities later.

Marco was a design student, using his expertise to design clear and detailed maps of various districts and posting them on social media. "Escape routes were drawn by the interior design publicity team. The young people didn't know where to go. Bigger sisters and brothers helped draw clear escape routes for them."

Thomas, an IT programmer, also reported, "I launched a 'deep blue'[1] (social media) group to infiltrate (the 'deep blue' camp), pretending to be a 'neutral blue'. Occasionally (I) would raise questions .... It was possible to have a discussion with those who were light blue and didn't have a deep understanding of the issue. (The goal was to influence their view.)"

In the evening of the Mid-Autumn Festival of 2019 (13th September), Mei and her friends went up to the Lion Rock Mountain to form a human chain with fellow supporters. 'Why did we climb up (the mountain)? In fact, I really felt I couldn't do much. (But) I could help with this." Although they felt they were not the police's target and they sometimes dressed up like residents in the neighbourhood backing up the protesters, the risk of being arrested was unavoidable. "My husband and I have made an agreement: we would not turn back to rescue the other because we have someone at home (their children) to take care of."

---

1   The pro-government sector was called the "blue camp", and anyone supporting it was a "blue ribbon". On the other hand, the anti-government and pro-democracy sector was called the "yellow camp", and its supporters "yellow ribbons".

4   We Are Here to Accompany the Young People

Cherry and her husband were both social workers. They chose to play the role of companion and someone to establish facts and get to the truth:

> On the night of August 31st, we were in Lai Chi Kok. But there were no injured people coming out (from the underground station). We saw an ambulance, but it left without rescuing anyone. I was very worried. Where were those people (who were injured)? ... Since that day, we had an idea of "guarding the truth". Truth is our last weapon .... Collaborating with the media, (we) looked for witnesses of the August 31st Incident. We looked for FAS (First-aiders, i.e., volunteer rescuers), the injured, fire-fighters, journalists, wanting to establish the truth .... We found out in this process that accompanying those witnesses or volunteer rescuers to talk about the incident and its development was also a healing process. Otherwise, they would continue to feel depressed and helpless. (If some-one kept them company,) they were able to get out of the dead alley.

Another task they took on with other social workers was to dialogue with the riot police on-site:

> We understand there was also a lot of pressure on the police, to the extent that their mental state was 'on red alert'. When we turned on the loud-speaker (to speak to them), we reminded them where their profession-alism lay. Their guidelines are: no hitting on the head, no shooting or lifting the gun when no one is charging. We announced these (guidelines) on the loudspeaker to remind those senior police officers and hoped to awaken them.

Elsa, a retired accountant, had no reservation in supporting the young protest-ers on the two university campuses – the Chinese University of Hong Kong and Hong Kong Polytechnic University. Self-identified as a PRN (peaceful, rational, non-violent), she had participated in the June 9th and 12th marches since the beginning and had ingested a lot of tear gas. Elsa and her teammates in the "Protect Our Kids" group had formed human chains separating the police and the protesters many times during the clashes. The team leader would then work with the social workers on-site to negotiate between the two camps. Often, they were able to gain trust from both sides and resolve the standoff.

On November 11th, Elsa and her teammates went to Bridge No. 2 in the Chinese University of Hong Kong (where the students' siege first began) and tried to advise the young people not to provoke the police. "They (the young people) had already set up their barricades at that time. It was very hard to convince them to leave. As our team leader said, young people had their own independent thinking. We could never tell them to retreat or direct any of their actions. We could only remind them that the riot police were in the area, the risk they needed to bear, and that they needed to have their own risk assessment .... Like in social work training, one would never suggest (that their clients) 'not' to do this, 'not' to do that. We hoped they would take great care and pay attention to safety."

Initially Elsa and her teammates wanted to communicate with the police supervisor, but the situation deteriorated rapidly. Then they themselves got trapped in danger. Later when the situation calmed down a bit, they went to the sports stadium to assist the first aid rescuers to wash the young people's eyes. "I then sat down and helped them wash (their eyes), as their elders, talking to them while washing (their eyes)."

On November 16th, an intense clash broke out between the police and the protesters in the Polytechnic University of Hong Kong. Elsa and her teammates– approximately 35–50 of them – entered the Polytechnic University campus in the afternoon on November 17th. At the peak of the clash, she and her teammates helped wash the young people who got hit by tear gas or water cannons. "We were in tears as we helped shower the bodies of those young people. Even though they were in immense pain, they were not afraid .... One of the young persons who came to let us help him wash had gotten hit by a water cannon three times. But he still had to go out again. He said, 'There were not enough people. The brothers out there could no longer fend off (the police).' Although we were in tears when we helped them wash, what else could we do in this movement? Watching how persistent those young people were, I felt I could die protecting these young people. Now that the young people could be so fearless, giving up their own future, what else was I afraid of?"

Elsa and the other 40–50 "Protect Our Kids" team members were arrested in the November clash in the Polytechnic University. Before taking off, the team leader had already told them that the risk of getting arrested this time was around 80–90%, saying that whoever wanted to leave could choose to leave first. Elsa reported, "In the end everyone stayed behind. We speculated that once arrested, (we) would be charged for obstructing police officers or for illegal gathering. Little could we imagine that we would be charged for riot ...."

FIGURE 8   Resisting police water cannons. In response to the HKUST student Chow Tsz-lok
            falling to his death (see footnote 2, Chap 3), protesters called for a series of actions
            on several days from November 11, 2019 onwards, which included citywide strikes,
            the occupation of the campus of the Polytechnic University and the blockade of
            the Cross Harbour Tunnel. The police deployed two water cannon vehicles and
            Unimog U5000 armoured personnel carriers on November 17 to enforce clearing
            and hold a siege of the campus. This picture was taken on the Cheong Wan Road
            flyover on November 17, 2019 when protesters were building a brick wall on the
            road to stop police from entering the campus of the Polytechnic University.

5   We Provide Legal Assistance and Do Fundraising

In addition to volunteering to drive protesters home and providing first aid
assistance, Sesame, a clerk, would also ask her lawyer friend to help look for
those young people who were arrested or missing. "If the young people whom
I knew went missing, (a lawyer friend) would help me look for them. Or before
I went out, I would ask her, 'hey, what's your risk assessment this time?' … This
friend knew people who took criminal cases. If I had a young person getting
into trouble, she would help refer (a lawyer). Or she would brief me on many
things. I would then tell the young person how to respond to the police."

Sheung worked in a law firm and had some legal knowledge. She would
actively explain to others the details of the Amendment Bill. "I would proac-
tively tell people as soon as I see them: friends' gatherings, at meals, family gatherings …. Later I installed TG (telegram) on my phone and joined roughly 20 TG

FIGURE 9   Petrol bombs against armoured cars. On November 17, 2019, protesters threw petrol bombs at a police armoured vehicle outside the Polytechnic University campus.

groups. By June 15th (or) 16th, when Lam-Cheng (Carrie Lam) announced postponing (the Extradition Amendment Bill), some people equated 'postponing' to 'withdrawing'. So, I sent out a detailed post in all my TG groups to explain the difference between 'postponement' and 'withdrawal' .... in case people were satisfied, thinking (wrongly) that (the Bill) was withdrawn."

Tam was arrested in Causeway Bay in November 2019. He had attended some training workshops provided by human rights lawyers in Hong Kong. He then believed that legal knowledge was important to protect himself as well as other young protesters. He said, "After arrest, I couldn't join the protest in the forefront, so I joined the legal support group to provide legal training for young people instead. They need to learn how to respond to the police, face interrogation in the police station, as well as prepare themselves to be in court. I already have the experience and the knowledge, and so I would like to share this with them."

Carmen, a retired lawyer, commented on the situation:

By August 31st, I sensed that (the situation) was very dangerous. What we were facing was a (powerful) regime, not an ordinary government.

> I participated in the movement but couldn't charge to the front. I mainly participated in fundraising and donations.

Many middle-aged participants, like Carmen, helped do fundraising for the movement. Amy, an engineer, said,

> I only participated that time (on June 16th). I didn't go to rallies afterwards because the situation was relatively dangerous. My participation was donation, that is donating quite a lot. I felt that since I dared not do things in the frontline, I could only donate .... Knowing about the CUHK incident (in November), I got very worried. As soon as I received the message .... that is, the young people there were trapped or something, I forwarded (the message) as much as I could to people whom I felt could be of help .... Tried my best to help! On the other hand, (I) educated my children at home to let them know about the whole situation. I would say more, talk about China, what the communist party is like, what Chinese people are like, etc. They are still young. I don't want to torment their thinking. But I want them to know a bit of the background so that they can think independently for themselves when the time comes.

Although the participants discussed in this section said they played the role of backup support in the movement, they occupied very different positions. Sending out messages or producing publicity materials on social media platforms, producing maps for the frontline protesters' safe escape, and providing legal assistance and fundraising among friends to support the frontline: all these could be carried out off-site. However, much of the backup support happened on-site, including first aid, supplies delivery, being a sentinel or a volunteer driver, staying behind on the scene as witness or to record events, protecting or accompanying young protesters, holding up opened umbrellas in the middle to front lines to help safeguard other protesters, and even negotiating between the riot police and the protesters. All these ran the risk of being injured or arrested. In fact, one of our respondents, Elsa, was arrested in the Polytechnic University clash. Even for the relatively 'safe' work of managing the Lennon Walls, several volunteers got attacked and injured.

CHAPTER 6

"Hong Kong" vs "Mainland China": Identity and Resistance

Despite multiple roles played in the Movement due to various reasons and capacities, a strong Hong Kong identity forms the basis of solidarity among the protesters and strengthens the sense of urgency of the Movement. Many interviewees saw the amendment of the extradition laws as destroying the "firewall" between the two places, thus exposing Hong Kong to serious challenges to its human rights, freedom and rule of law. Failure to protest or to persevere would result in the diminishing of existing values such as freedom of speech, and Hong Kong would slowly become mainland China. Others worried that the situation would become even worse: that Hong Kong would succumb to the iron-fisted suppression of the Chinese Communist Party (CCP), just as Xinjiang now was. The words "What Xinjiang was yesterday is Hong Kong today" express their fear in this regard.

Our interviewees defined Hong Kong identity mainly through the fundamental differences they saw between the social institutions and values of Hong Kong and mainland China, as well as irreconcilable cultural clashes between these two places. To them, identification with Hong Kong came with core values which include: an aspiration for freedom of speech and thought, separation of powers, respect of truth, a clean government, sanctity of contract, free flow of communication, etc. Not only that, but it also meant a lifestyle with which they were already familiar. Adopting an entirely different Chinese one meant not only having to give up the values they held dear, but also succumbing to a lifestyle which they detested. When the HKSAR government proceeded to amend the extradition laws, they therefore understood this move as dismantling the legal firewall which had been protecting the institutions and values of Hong Kong from infiltration by the mainland Chinese ones. This, to them, amounted to a serious challenge of their unique identity, and in this context, the strong resistance they put up becomes understandable.

Nevertheless, quite a few acknowledged that they were Chinese, in terms of culture, ethnicity and blood. What they did not identify with was the Chinese Communist Party. Others thought that they were both Hongkongers *and* Chinese, Hong Kong being a part of China. Yet others were convinced that Chinese culture has its value, and the country is magnificent and beautiful, but these had nothing to do with supporting the Chinese Communist Party. To them, the ruling Party and the country were two separate entities and should not be confused. Loving the country does not mean loving the Party: it is not that they did not accept their Chinese identity, but that they did not approve of, nor accept, the Communist regime and its ideas. They believed that once they accepted it, the values and lifestyle of Hong Kong, held dear by its residents, would diminish.

Admittedly, some of our interviewees held anti-Mainlanders feelings, believing that the latter, whether new immigrants, or tourists who came to purchase goods, infringed on the interests of Hongkongers. They believed that new immigrants strained the locals' resources, such as lengthening the queue for public housing, reducing their schooling and employment opportunities, etc. As for the visitors, they brought inconveniences to daily life, such as causing serious congestion in areas where parallel traders and mainland tourists gathered. Apart from these, some interviewees believed the SAR government privileged new immigrants and Mainland undertakings through their policies. They also believed that numerous benefits were transferred to Mainland enterprises through major infrastructure construction projects. Deepening contradictions between Hong Kong and mainland China thus further sharpen the identity conflict. For example, Jack, a driver, said:

> (We) are like a collective body. Why calling them (other protesters) as *sau zuk*? Why saying 'not leaving anyone behind' (in the protest scenes)? This is the identity of Hongkonger. They saw protesters being beaten up by the police. They felt they were part of the collective. So, they wanted revenge.

The collective body was built on a sense of collective identity as Hongkonger. But to Brick, who just graduated from university, the discernment and recognition of the Hongkonger identity did not emerge from behind closed doors. Rather, it was a result of her participation in public protests.

> Hong Kong has not had a subjective agency for many years. Economic success cannot define our generation. What our generation yearn for is not material things .... 'Who are you?' .... 'Why do you exist here?', etc. During the 2014 Umbrella Movement you still could not define what a Hongkonger was. It was really until the 2016 Fish Ball Revolution[1] that (we) realised .... At least we have this characteristic in our generation. We

---

1   See p.148, Chapter 13.

wanted to define ourselves .... (through) pursuing a particular value or
being persistent in our character, at least in these issues of great impor-
tance to us ... that already makes a difference. ... A subjective consciousness and how I define this place ... how to define myself .... In this way,
what (I was fighting for) defines me.

> Brick, university graduate

1   Foundation of Identity: Political and Social Values

Identity and social movement are mutually constitutive and are cause and
effect of each other. As mentioned above, many respondents got involved
in this movement to stop the Extradition Amendment Bill and prevent connecting Hong Kong's legal system to China's to allow the transfer of fugitives
to Mainland China. Therefore, protesters also called this Movement "Against
Transfer to Mainland China Movement". The premise of "Against Transfer to
Mainland China" was that Hong Kong and Mainland China must be separated
by a political "firewall". The goal of "Against Transfer to Mainland China" was to
safeguard this political "firewall" between Hong Kong and Mainland China and
to keep the two legal systems separate. However, according to many respondents, there was another consideration of deeper implications behind safeguarding this firewall. That was the separation of the Hong Kong identity from
that of Mainland China. This unique identity was built on the vast difference
between Hong Kong and Mainland China in their political system and values.
Kiki, a secondary school student said,

> (In Hong Kong) you are exposed to a lot of information. This feels very
> different from Mainland China .... Hong Kong is inclusive of different
> cultures, different religions, and ideas. China has very little tolerance for
> religion. It often promotes personal idolisation .... In terms of freedom of
> speech, writing posts on WeChat could be banned in China. But Chinese
> people are used to it. Hong Kong is not like that.

To many participants, the three concepts, culture, country and the ruling
party, had to be distinguished. Terry, the young traditional Chinese medicine
practitioner who conceived Hong Kong as part of Chinese culture, further
explained,

> I would not say out loud that I am Chinese or Hongkonger. But Hong
> Kong culture is Waa-jan (Sino) culture. (We) speak Chinese, write

Chinese, read (Chinese) poetry, song lyrics, and history. In fact, China has several thousand years of history. It's not just 70 years of nation building. Therefore, I am a ... Waa-jan, but I do not want to have any relationship with the communist party. (I) have heard from a lot of people who seemed to be communist party members that voting within the party was all internally determined. Then in some remote city, a group of young people were locked up due to some multilevel direct marketing matter. You must have some connection to help you look around to spot (locate) them. Only then can you rescue them. The local police would not help you or solve the case even if they might have already known something happened. Probably even the police would profit (from what happened) behind the scenes ... (That is, for those issues that involve triad society networks ... it's useless to report to the police.) Therefore, I think (the Extradition Amendment Bill) cannot be accepted. That is "Transfer to Mainland China" would transfer whoever the authority does not like up there ... in whatever way they like.

Another secondary school student, King Carp, who had sympathy with grassroot people in mainland China, also expressed her worry:

When I was in Form 3 (Year 9), we studied the Opening-up Policy (in Liberal Studies) and the issue of *sannong* (the three major issues of peasants, rural villages, and agriculture). I quite liked it and felt close to China .... Why did the (Chinese) government make their people live like that? I felt that they (people in China) were very miserable! We watched different video-clips in class which showed us what it was like there. Why did the authorities treat them (people) like that? If they would do that even to their own people, what about Hong Kong? What can we do? ... Some classmates cried watching (those clips).

Steve, an advertising worker whose family had a factory in Mainland China, also observed the unacceptable arbitrary power and corruption in the country. He said,

My father was responsible for managing the business (of our relative's factory in Mainland China). He learnt about a lot of unreasonable things there. Our surname is the same as that of the city mayor. (We) also originated from the same village. Because of this, (my father) got a lot of 'conveniences', such as sailing through bureaucratic formalities, getting approval, or extra help. I remember one time my father went through customs with a vase. The customs officer said it was a national protected cultural item and would detain him. In fact, it was a very ordinary vase. But after my father called the city mayor to ask him to help solve the issue, he was released in 10 minutes. Since I was small, (my father) had told us about many things like that.

But there are also some extreme cases in which anti-China sentiments were severe. Winnie, who was not willing to disclose her occupation, said,

(My) view about China is not too different from that of North Korea. Both are very dictatorial and closed countries but (China) did better on appearance. Of course, China's economy is better ... but, it's very bad in regard to freedom. I went with classmates to join the June 4th rally (regarding Tiananmen Square massacre in 1989) in junior high and learnt, wow, this was what China did! I studied humanities, Chinese history ... about the history of the 20th century. When studying the Cultural Revolution, I felt it was outrageous. This country was like that. Therefore, I haven't had a good impression (of China) since I was small. As I grew up, I knew China had done so much: for example, Liu Xiaobo, I paid close attention ... the artist Ai Weiwei, I also paid close attention .... knowing how they were oppressed. Or Li Wangyang,[2] I was very angry at the time .... (in my) teenage years .... the Li Wangyang incident made me feel not wanting to go to the Mainland anymore. China will not change. It will always be under one-party authoritarian rule.

Like Winnie, Dove also commented,

---

2   Li Wangyang had been imprisoned for 22 years for organising workers' participation in the Democracy Movement in Hunan in 1989. When he was freed in 2011, he was already deaf and blind from his deprivations and possibly serious torture in prison. Yet, when he was interviewed by a Hong Kong reporter from Cable TV in 2012, he said adamantly, "I wouldn't turn back even if my head was chopped off". Four days after the report was aired, Li was reported dead from hanging in hospital. The government insisted that he committed suicide, but this was refuted by his family and the public. A protest march took place in Hong Kong, demanding the Chinese government to investigate the real cause of his death. See "Hong Kong Media: Li Wangyang's family has never agreed to 'Suicide'", BBC Chinese, 12 Sept 2012, https://www.bbc.com/zhongwen/trad/chinese_news/2012/09/120912_china_li (in Chinese, last viewed 9 Sept 2022); "The Li Wangyang Incident", U-Beat Magazine, School of Journalism and Communication, The Chinese University of Hong Kong, 3 Jan 2014, https://tinyurl.com/2p5s425w (in Chinese, last viewed 9 Sept 2022).

There were a lot of lies in what the Chinese Communist Party said ... I feel China must go through a baptism of democracy to allow people to have a choice.

Dove, occupation not identified

Many participants had work or business experience in Mainland China, which laid the foundation for their poor impressions on the country. As Henry, a clerk, said,

Because of my previous job, (I) was always in China .... have never liked it there. I have always felt that the methods they (people in power) used were so much more astute than us "Hong Kong people". We are very fragile, not far-sighted and prudent enough.

Jack, the driver, also openly stated that he did not want to be identified as Chinese. He said,

To be honest, it is difficult (for me) to identify as Chinese. It is even worse now .... I have a friend working in the university who got scolded out of the blue (by someone from the Mainland), saying that Hongkongers were fighting for Hong Kong independence, and were organising a revolution. The information they (people in China) receive is different from what we receive here. Simply put, they are too brainwashed .... (Despite this) there are still a lot of conscientious Mainlanders. Otherwise, there won't be so many human rights defenders who got arrested.

Ka-ming, the university student, also commented,

We are Hongkongers. (To protest) is not for money. It's not for anything but purely for the core value of democracy in our fight to date. In a way, we are very romantic. (My mother) told me adamantly not to go out again. I said I must go out for the future. My family are Mainlanders. My grandfather applied to come to Hong Kong, then my father was born in the Mainland .... You came to Hong Kong for a better life. Why would you give up now?

The family (reunited) when my mother sponsored my father's entry to Hong Kong. But my father still worked in the Mainland. In fact, I have a lot of cultural experience in Hong Kong and China. (I was born in Hong Kong and studied kindergarten in the Mainland). I feel that Hong Kong has the three core values of the rule of law, (democracy and freedom).

China doesn't have it at all. This is indispensable in Hong Kong but is now
being shattered, such as the separation of powers (executive, legislative,
judicial). This is unacceptable. Precisely because of this, I have fought
with my father .... I totally despise the Mainland's public security system
because I have seen too much (corruption) in my home village.

Ka-ming could not stop herself and further explained,

My uncle in the Mainland plays both the black and white sides (the criminal and official sides). That is, he can bribe the police because he has
relatives working in the government. His power in the criminal force is
also very strong. Indeed, he 'plays it all'.

Living in both places has affected Ka-ming's personal development in many
ways. The most obvious is the matter of identity. She explained that she could
not differentiate Hongkonger and Chinese when she was in kindergarten in
China. Gradually, however, she began to discern the differences. She realised
that the Mainland was fundamentally different, especially in terms of values,
after she came to Hong Kong and received a lot of critical thinking education.
She said,

It has made me think a lot. Ultimately, people need to have basic cour-
tesy, to believe in social justice, to believe that the law of natural justice
is like a giant web, although sparsely meshed, nothing can slip through.

Terry, the traditional Chinese medicine practitioner, had lived in some major
cities in China for several years due to his study and work. He therefore felt the
same way as Ka-ming. He had direct experience of China's society. He felt that
the Chinese political system had distorted human nature and that misguided
patriotic sentiments could easily make people accept unjust situations in the
society. He recalled one incident while he was living in a major Chinese city,

Where my friend worked was a very central location. People around were
all OL (office ladies). It's not a poor or remote area or a place with no
culture. But one time she was hit by a car. No one dared to pick her up
or help her .... Fortunately, I happened to be in the area. Immediately,
I went to find (her). (She) was lying in the middle of the road. But no
one dared to make a phone call in a big city, at a central location, a place
where people had a certain level of education. ... I couldn't accept it. Why
was it that when people needed mutual help, the system there couldn't

protect those who helped others, who wanted to be someone with a conscience? ... They (colleagues and supervisors in China) recalled the 2014 Umbrella Movement and thought that Hongkongers were bad. I felt this was ridiculous. They didn't know what had happened at all. But there was really no way (to tell them what happened) because the authorities (in China) controlled the news and asserted that it was a plot for "Hong Kong Independence" and that it could not even be discussed .... They would sing their praises for what the Communist Party has given them (but I) felt that they knew in their hearts the flaws of the authorities, including things like toxic baby formula and toxic vaccines. In fact, they really know. But when an outsider mentions these things – Hongkonger is half an outsider to them – they would feel like they are losing face .... It's okay to talk about it among themselves. But outsiders are not allowed to comment, regardless of how reasonable their words might be. (They) need to save face.

Most respondents emphasised social or political values as the foundation of the "Hongkonger" identity. This is what some of them said:

I was very surprised by an incident posted on Lihkg (a popular discussion online forum among protesters in 2019). A protester was found to be a Mainlander. (Then I) realised that as long as (someone) identifies with Hong Kong values, we all consider them as a Hongkonger. This was a consensus. This was quite different from before. Of course, Leung Tin-kei's[3] mother is also a Mainlander. He (Leung) was born in China.

Even though both Leung Tin-kei and Law Kwun Chung[4] were born in the Mainland, their birthplace does not represent the stand they take.

---

3   Edward Leung (Chinese: Leung Tin-kei), born in Wuhan in 1991, grew up in Hong Kong and was a member of Hong Kong Indigenous, which advocated for Hong Kong self-determination. Leung was arrested in February 2016 for his participation in the "Mongkok Unrest" (also known as "Fish Ball Revolution"). Convicted of rioting and assaulting a police officer, he was sentenced to jail for six years. Leung was released from prison in January 2022 and must currently observe a supervision order.

4   Nathan Law (Chinese: Law Kwun-chung), born in Shenzhen in 1993 and raised in Hong Kong since around 6 years old, participated in the 2014 Umbrella Movement as Secretary-General of the Hong Kong Federation of Students (HKFS). He founded the political party, Demosistō, with Joshua Wong and Agnes Chow in 2016, was elected as the Legislative Councillor representing the Hong Kong Island District and became the youngest Legislative Councillor in Hong Kong history. Law went to the United States to lobby for sanctions against China in 2019. He went into exile in the UK before the Hong Kong National Security Law came into effect in July 2020. He has since been actively involved in overseas lobbying work.

There is also Liu Xiaobo, Chen Guangcheng,[5] and Chen Qiushi[6] in the Mainland, who were/are also very awake, knowledgeable persons with ideals. Shouldn't assume other people's stand and whether they have conscience based on where they were born. Birthplace is not a choice, but conscience is.

Grace, Chinese enterprise employee

The emphasis on cultural value and not birthplace as an important element of Hong Kong local identity illustrates that this resistance movement has gone beyond a single political agenda to become a cultural identity movement. Indeed, to many participants, this movement was an important process of identity formation.

2 Rejecting Immigrants and Tourists from China and Objecting to Profit Transfer to China

As one can see above, the "Hongkonger" identity was mostly constructed in contrast to Mainland China. Other than talking about the differences in the political system and social values between the two places and hence cherishing what Hong Kong had, some interviewees also directly expressed xenophobic sentiments and displeasure with new immigrants and tourists from China, feeling that the former had thinned the resources Hongkongers originally had while the latter had caused inconvenience in their daily lives. Being influenced by xenophobic views in some major newspapers, Lam, the salesperson, held a distorted picture and commented.

New immigrants can move to public housing fast. Hongkongers don't get that.

---

5 Chen Guangcheng, visually impaired, is a self-taught lawyer. After he organised a lawsuit against the local authorities in Linyi, Shandong in 2005, he was placed under house arrest and then formal arrest. He was then sentenced to four years in prison. After having served his sentence, he was placed under house arrest again. In 2012, he escaped and fled to the US Embassy in Beijing. After some negotiations, his wife and children were granted visas to the US in 2012. In 2013, he was able to leave China and was sent to the US.

6 Chen Qiushi is a lawyer, activist, and citizen journalist. He covered the 2019 protests in Hong Kong, and the COVID-19 outbreak in Wuhan, being very critical of the authorities' response to the epidemic. He went missing in February 2020, but re-emerged in September 2021, yet giving no explanation for his disappearance.

Some protesters would even say,

> We (speak) Cantonese. Why the necessity to accommodate their needs (to speak Putonghua in university classes)? Why not respect our culture? ... Some new immigrants say it's hard to live in a partitioned flat. Then why do they come here?
>
> Marco, university student

Problematic localism also fuelled the participants to believe that the Mainlanders came to Hong Kong to create severe competition in social resources and the job market. Bak, a secondary school student said,

> There are too many Mainlanders (in Hong Kong), often thinning the resources. For example, Hong Kong degrees (should) be reserved to Hong Kong citizens, those born in Hong Kong. The competition for education in Hong Kong has increased. So is the competition for jobs upon graduation. Perhaps because of this, there are more unemployed, or not having the opportunity to further study .... They (new immigrants) get Hong Kong citizen status after living here for 7 years .... and can compete for resources as a Hongkonger: job, degree, housing, etc. But they are not locally born and raised.

Forgetting that Hong Kong is a mobile and migrant society, Winnie, an accountant who participated in the Movement also commented,

> Lam Cheng Yuet-ngor's (the Chief Executive of HKSAR government) proposal of raising the mortgage cap for first-time buyers was all for the people in China. To build an artificial island is also for the people in China. It's the same with the public housing and home-ownership-scheme flats given to new immigrants. I think the policy of raising the mortgage cap is fundamentally toxic. Condo prices increased significantly as soon as the policy was announced. One unit in Lung Mun Oasis in Tuen Mun has increased by one million (HK dollars). It's not about helping young people come on board to own their property. It's helping those Mainlanders who already own flat units to sell their property at the highest price in order to withdraw their assets.

Besides, Jack the driver also talked about the property speculation activities of Mainlanders in Hong Kong and his view on the Hong Kong Government's profit transfer to Mainland enterprises: "The housing issue is too difficult to solve .... The Government should build more public housing. Flats are so expensive now due to Mainlanders' property speculation. Reviewing the history since the sovereignty return (in 1997), (we) have often seen that the final cost of every project exceeded 1–2 times of the budget. It's all capital transfer back to the Mainland. All projects are conducted by Chinese enterprises. It is profit transfer."

3   Between Chinese and Hong Kong Identity

Some respondents expressed their displeasure with new immigrants and tourists from China. But many moved back and forth between their Chinese and Hong Kong identity. Some articulated more clearly that what they could not accept was not the Chinese identity, but the communist rule and the resulting socio-political climate. Kei, the IT worker, has a more complicated view concerning the Chinese and Hong Kong identity. He said,

> (I) have been feeling more unhappy (since the protest movement). I feel that people on the other side (mainland Chinese) are clearly of the same racial ethnicity as mine. But why don't I want to ... be identified as coming from the same race? ... In fact, like us in Hong Kong, people in Taiwan have also inherited Sino-culture. But we don't have the capacity to change the Chinese Government .... Perhaps part of our Chinese culture is worth promoting and to be transmitted to the next generation. But unfortunately, we're not able to do so. It's very sad to get discriminated against when (we) travel overseas (being mistaken to be coming from mainland China).

We have seen earlier that the Hongkonger identity involves an identification with certain values, and this brings into focus the dual goal of the Anti-ELAB Movement: defending the institutions and core values of Hong Kong, and revisiting values which are worth holding onto but which might soon disappear, so that one might rebuild Hong Kong. Many participants were able to highlight the differences among the culture, the country, and the party, and they also stressed their identification with the culture and the country. Cindy, a retired worker also said,

> We are of Chinese blood lineage. This definitely can't be changed. But if you say we should follow China, follow the Chinese Communist Party, their ideology, for Hongkongers, no! At least I can't. The Hongkonger

identity is recognised globally .... local born and raised, ideas, the idea of freedom, the idea of citizenship. These are all Hongkongers' values.

Loafer, the university student, tried to make a distinction between the country and the party. He commented,

> I love the country but not the political party. I like China .... Huaxia (Sino) civilisation has interested many people. You see many foreigners deliberately come to China to learn about its history because this is a very attractive country, with beautiful places, such as the step fields in Yunnan, etc. I like this place, I like this country. But the communist party is destroying this place, this country. If the Mainland does not adopt communism .... (but) adopts democracy, that is so much better: more freedom, we would be willing to go with one country, one system or a federal government system like the United States.

Chubby Cockroach, a clerk, also said he was fine with both the identity of Hongkonger and Chinese.

> I say I am a Hongkonger. But if you ask me if I am Chinese, I will also say I am. One can't deny that Hong Kong is indeed part of China. Secondly, I also feel much of Chinese culture is quite good, other than the political aspect. Sometimes I also read Chinese history. I don't particularly like it, but would not deny that I am Chinese. I have studied Chinese history at school and have read some information after I started to work. I appreciate ancient Chinese thoughts. They are indeed profound. There's no reason why I don't like these things because of political reasons. Besides, I do truly feel that Hong Kong is part of China. Talking about two systems, why can't I have two identities: Hongkonger as well as Chinese?

4   "Today's Xinjiang, Tomorrow's Hong Kong"

As mentioned above, protesters demanded a full withdrawal of the Extradition Bill Amendment, an independent commission of inquiry into alleged police brutality, and dual universal suffrage (including both the Legislative Council and the Chief Executive), and so on. However, other than these concrete demands, the identification with "Hong Kong" as a collective was also tangibly and dynamically present, re-established, and consolidated in this Movement.

This identity was formed in contrast to the identification with "China". Nevertheless, the displeasure the respondents aforementioned had towards the new immigrants from China seems to have been a longstanding sentiment. Similarly, the negative perception and experience many respondents had towards the Chinese Communist Party regime and the resulting socio-political culture did not emerge overnight. In 2019, however, there was a strong feeling of urgency and determination.

> If we don't come out to protest, really .... yesterday's Xinjiang is today's Hong Kong.
>
> Elf, shop assistant

> If we don't fight today, freedom of speech or information on the internet, Hong Kong will gradually become today's China. Hong Kong didn't report any further news about the incinerators built in Wuhan[7] because of a government crackdown .... Our thinking is that Xinjiang is our future. If we don't fight, we will become Xinjiang.
>
> Lam, salesperson

> I am worried that Hong Kong would be like Xinjiang .... Hongkongers are so involved now because the government is constantly testing Hongkongers' bottom line. Since you (the government) don't budge, we will also not concede.
>
> Steve, advertising worker

Summarising what the respondents said about the Chinese and Hongkonger identities, we can see the characteristics of this "Against Transfer to China Movement". On the one hand, it was a defensive movement: to protect Hong Kong so that it would not lose the freedom and civilised system and culture which it originally had. To a certain extent, there were also some xenophobic elements against people from Mainland China. On the other hand, however, it was also a constructive movement: to re-embody some values that were worth preserving but were in the process of being lost. These were the values that were dynamically constructed in the process of the movement. As Zoe said:

---

7   There was news about local residents' protests against the building of new incinerators in a district in the city of Wuhan. These protests were, however, suppressed after a week or so, and reports about them were quickly censored. See "Wuhan protests: Incinerator plan sparks mass unrest", BBC News, 8 July 2019. https://www.bbc.com/news/blogs-china-blog-48904350 (last viewed 23 Sept 2022).

To me, being Hongkonger means that she/he should be living in Hong Kong, getting involved in things happening in Hong Kong, identifying with some Hong Kong values, and having the obligation to do something for Hong Kong. It could be people of different skin colour, different social strata. But values are what is more important .... In fact, I don't deny I am Chinese. ... I don't mind calling myself Chinese .... (However) I now have a new Hongkonger's identity, having experienced our solidarity in this Anti-ELAB Movement. During this movement, there is a new value identification ... (New Hongkongers) are braver than before, reasonable, fact-finding, logical, acting in accordance with (fact, evidence, reason), and in stronger solidarity. In the past, (Hongkongers) were probably more selfish. Now (people) come out not only for their own self-interest. Once having come forward, it's not one's own business any more, but that of a collective. Enough strength is needed to achieve certain things.

CHAPTER 7

What It Means

Through the voices, experiences, and reflections of 56 participants in the Anti-ELAB Movement, we have tried to explore their original intentions and motivations, their considerations concerning their roles and choices, their political claims, visions, identities, and emotions. We also try to illustrate their judgments on the current situation, their understanding of the Movement, as well as the expectations they held for themselves, and from these, we hope to contribute to the comprehension of the origins, motivations, and changes of this Movement.

1   Political Motivation

From our interviewees' recapitulations of their experiences, we could see that the Anti-ELAB Movement had been propelled by what the HKSAR government had done or refused to do. Our interviewees had joined the Movement for only one reason: their dissatisfaction with the government's decision to amend the relevant law, which would then make possible for "fugitives" in Hong Kong to be extradited to Mainland China Even so, when the Amendment Bill was proposed in mid-February 2019, only a minority of our interviewees had realised the gravity of the issue and joined the Movement. By May of the same year, when political arguments in the Legislative Council intensified and physical scuffles occurred, the legal procedure was stalled and only at this point did the incident attract public attention. Even then, however, the government refused to negotiate with different political parties to find a common ground. Instead, it announced that the second reading of the Bill would resume in full council on 12th June, thus bypassing the Bills Committee and sabotaging the normal procedure. This move amounted to announcing a non-negotiable date for the Bill to go through, and this naturally intensified political mobilisation and amplified the voices of the opposition. Amidst numerous joint signature campaigns and protesting actions our interviewees felt the rising heat: from first paying attention to the issue, to understanding what was going on; and then from this, they realised that the time for action had arrived. Three days before the legislative process was to resume, the Civil Human Rights Front organised a mass protest rally on 9th June, and it was on this day that many protesters came out and "walked" for the first time.

Even then, our interviewees had not held high hopes for the protest. Some said they came out just to express their dissatisfaction, not having considered its impact. Others said they would call it a day if the government had made small concessions. Apart from a small minority, most of our interviewees did not have the slightest hope, not to say determination, of stalling the legislative process through their action. Nevertheless, most of our interviewees could not have anticipated that the government would totally disregard the high turnout of over a million protesters that day and not back down even for an inch, and even worse, that it would make a public announcement that the legislative process would proceed on the designated date, even before the protesters had dispersed. With shock and anger, they realised that much greater determination and commitment was needed if the Amendment Bill was to be stalled. As a result, thousands of citizens surrounded the Legislative Council on 12th June, and the Council meeting had to be adjourned.

Although our interviewees saw their initial goal achieved, yet the Movement continued. The unexpectedly high-handed suppression tactics on 12th June failed to stop the protesters. Instead, these just pushed the protest movement to a higher level. The countless rounds of bullets not only caused direct injuries, but also a near fatal stampede. Some of our interviewees caught in this frightful incident were overwhelmed by a deep sense of injustice and helplessness, as well as shock and anger. Much to their astonishment, the police showed no regrets at all. Rather, they publicly declared soon after that this protest was a "riot", and the participants were "rioters". This precipitated the tragedy of Mr. Leung Ling-kit, who, on June 15th, had strongly remonstrated with the threat of suicide, and who, sadly, fell to his death afterwards. Mr. Leung's death shocked many of our interviewees, and their determination to fight grew. Leung's death completely overshadowed the government's decision to suspend the Bill that day, and the scheduled protest rally on the next day, entitled "Condemn Suppression, Withdraw the Iniquitous Bill", drew an unprecedentedly high attendance of 2 million. For our interviewees, the protest movement had to be escalated, with their dissatisfaction with government's attempt to amend the Bill now intensifying to frustration with police brutality and the imperviousness of the government, who had now descended to using police brutality to expedite poor governance.

2   Radicalisation of the Movement and Changes in Participants' Roles

For our interviewees, police brutality was the key factor behind the antagonism between government and the people, as well as the driving force for the

Movement's escalation. The police brutality they themselves had suffered, or had witnessed, not only jolted their assumptions and feelings, but it also drove them to reevaluate the nature of the government and the direction of the Movement, and to decide on their own commitment and role. More specifically, police brutality fuelled participants' commitment, taking the Movement to a higher level.

Our interviews consistently showed that police brutality was the most common, most deeply felt and significant experience of the participants. Some of them were left with a sense of injustice and unfairness, others felt insult, anger, and incredulousness, yet others felt guilt (for other protesters' arrest and/ or injuries) and hatred. However, none of them chose to retreat, but instead resolved to join the Movement with greater resolution, either taking up a supportive role, or even joining the frontlines.

The acceleration of the Movement meant not only more serious confrontations, but also escalation of political demands: from withdrawal of the Amendment Bill to realising "dual universal suffrage", i.e., universal suffrage for election of Legislative Councillors and of the Chief Executive. These demands had grown not only from the participants' lived experience in the protests, but also from their assessment of the political situation as well as the core values they held. Many of them said that what they went through in the protests showed them that the socio-political system was in tatters, the government was totally unresponsive to society, and that the police no longer safeguarded the social order. In a nutshell, their vision for a society governed by the rule of law and a government subject to check-and-balance was now rapidly fading.

Yet, our interviewees believed that society could only get back on the right track if a democratic system was in place. They believed that with "dual universal suffrage", a democratic system complete with a healthy check-and-balance of power would come about. Only then would the government concede to an independent inquiry, as well as respond to the other demands. Only then, too, would the rule of law be restored, and would justice, freedom and a good livelihood be safeguarded. As a result, most people put "dual universal suffrage" above the others in their "Five Demands". In the words of two of our interviewees, a government mandated by popular choice was the "protection shield" of Hong Kong, ensuring that we would not be put at the mercy of others, most notably, the Chinese Communist rulers. For them, democracy is of a practical rather than spiritual value, and the Anti-Extradition Movement, through striving for "dual universal suffrage", was aimed more at defending an existing structure rather than building a new one.

FIGURE 10   Netizens organize march. On Halloween, October 31, 2019, some netizens
organized Masquerade Halloween and called on people to march from Victoria
Park in Causeway Bay to Lan Kwai Fong in Central. Citizens dressed up in
various costumes or wore character masks of senior Chinese and Hong Kong
officials. They chanted slogans, protesting the Hong Kong government's forced
implementation of the *Prohibition on Face Covering Regulation* and mourning the
831 Incident. Police suddenly blocked off Lan Kwai Fong that night, evacuated the
area by force and arrested many people.

Sadly, their hopes were crushed, and the draconian National Security Law
(Hong Kong)[1] was passed in late June 2020 by the Standing Committee of the
National People's Congress instead. The first person prosecuted under this law
was Tong Ying-kit. On 1st July that year, he drove his motorcycle with a banner
flying at the rear, which read: "Liberate Hong Kong, Revolution of Our Times",[2]
ran into three police officers, and was arrested. After having been detained for

---

1   The official title is Law of the People's Republic of China on Safeguarding National Security
     in the Hong Kong Special Administrative Region.
2   In the Movement, the most commonly used English translation of this slogan was: "Liberate
     Hong Kong, Revolution of Our Times", or "Free Hong Kong, Revolution Now". This slogan
     was used by Edward Leung Tin-kei of Hong Kong Indigenous when he ran for the Legislative
     Council by-election (New Territories East) in January 2016. In February that year, he was
     arrested for participating in the so-called "Fish Ball Revolution" in Mongkok, a case of social
     unrest ignited over defence of the rights of hawkers selling on the streets during Chinese New
     Year holidays. He eventually lost the election, though netting a high return. He was convicted

a year, Tong appeared in court for the first time on 8th April 2021, and he was eventually convicted of incitement to secession and committing acts of terror, and hence sentenced to a total of nine years.[3] After the enactment of the National Security Law, the slogan aforementioned, which had often appeared in the Anti-ELAB Movement, suddenly became taboo, signifying a serious crime and even the unspeakable capital offence of promulgating Hong Kong independence. Reading through our interviewees' transcripts concerning this slogan, however, we found nothing near to "incitement to secession and committing acts of terror". To them, "liberate Hong Kong" expressed a wish to restore the sound socio-political system and the rule of law that Hong Kong once had, as well as the democracy promised by the Basic Law. In particular, it expressed a wish to reinstate a police force with high professional standards. These words of one of our interviewees, Sheung, are representative of this view:

> (On the meaning of the slogan) Go back to the prosperous times Hong Kong once enjoyed, a sound political system and the rule of law. ... Go back to a highly reputable, peaceful ... a reputation attributable to the best police force in the world.

As for "Revolution of Our Times", none of the interviewees said it meant a replacement or supersession of the political regime. On the contrary, a few interviewees said the following:

> (it means) just reform of the times, not a revolution against the regime.
>> Thomas, an artist

> I think independence is not feasible. You can see that people don't really want independence; in fact, they still think Hong Kong is an inseparable part of China. But they do want more freedom for themselves. ...

---

of rioting and sentenced to 6 years imprisonment in June 2018. He was, therefore, absent from rallies and events during the Anti-Extradition Movement when his slogan was used.

3 See "First National Security Law Case: Prosecution's expert Lau Chi-pang: Riding a motorcycle with the 'Liberate Hong Kong, Revolution of Our Times' banner was like Charging a Horse with an Ensign to the Battlefield", *Standnews*, 8 April 2021 (web news no longer available). See also "Activist Tong Ying-kit jailed for nine years in Hong Kong's first national security case", *Hong Kong Free Press*, 30 July 2021. https://hongkongfp.com/2021/07/30/breaking-activist-tong-ying-kit-jailed-for-9-years-in-hong-kongs-first-national-security-case/ (last viewed 13 Sept 2022).

'Revolution of our times' is, just (literally) revolution of our times, a feeling that we have been selected (by our era) to encounter these happenings.

Amy, an engineer

'Revolution', I don't think Hong Kong can become independent. I don't support independence for Hong Kong. I guess there are a lot of objective reasons why Hong Kong independence cannot come about. The words 'Our times' contain an element of fate. ... 'Our times' denotes kind of a feeling of accepting one's fate, or not accepting one's fate. Or it is just the timing (she used English for this word): that these events happen just at this time.

Cherry, a social worker

No matter what the pro-government camp says about the 2019 Movement being "(instigated by) Black thugs" or "Colour revolution", that it wanted to promulgate Hong Kong Independence, subvert the HKSAR government or even the People's Republic of China regime, these have not emerged in our interviews at all. What our interviewees said, in fact, matched the testimony given by the two expert witnesses invited by the defence lawyer in Tong Ying-kit's case. One of them, Prof Eliza Wing-yee Lee, analysed the archival data concerning Edward Leung Tin-kei's usage of the slogan and came up with the interpretation as follows:

The political message conveyed by 'Recover Hong Kong, Revolution of Our Times' is this: 'reinstate the old order we have lost, unify people of all ages who love freedom, and bring about historical changes in a key moment'.[4]

3   Emotions and Feelings Driving the Movement

There were both rational and emotional reasons behind our interviewees' participation in the Movement. Rational considerations include the following: oppose the amendment of the extradition laws, realise the "Five Demands", defend the Hong Kong identity, etc. As for the emotional side, our

---

4 Yeung Tze-kei, "Notes on the First National Security Law case, no.1. Debate Among the Academics Over the Meaning of 'Recover' and 'Revolution', *Standnews*, 10 July 2021. https://bit.ly/3c6mSNa (no longer available).

FIGURE 11   Rally in Edinburgh Square. On the night of November 28, 2019, the Hong
Kong Higher Institutions International Affairs Delegation and Civic Group for
Thanksgiving Day Assembly jointly held a rally in Edinburgh Square, Central to
express their gratitude to the US Congress for passing the Hong Kong Human
Rights and Democracy Act and to President Donald Trump for signing it into
law. A protester was waving a "Free Hong Kong, Revolution Now" flag against a
backdrop of skyscrapers in Central.

interviewees recounted how their experience in the protests generated feelings and emotions that were deeply moving and simply ineradicable. These, in turn, became the motivating force behind their continuing participation in the Movement.

Our interviewees experienced both positive and negative emotions. Negative emotions were shock, fear and even hatred, generated mainly by personally experiencing or observing acts of injustice being committed. A common example of these was anxiety and fear arising from experiencing or witnessing violent suppression of protesters by the riot police. These then led to strong feelings of repugnance and anger, which, in turn, fuelled their determination to reclaim justice. Another negative emotion was guilt and shame, experienced mostly by adults or the aged who saw young people joining the Movement with enthusiasm, doing what they themselves would like to do but dared not do, and suffering serious consequences as a result. This guilt urged them on to do more of what they could, within the limits of the risks they could take. Other interviewees suffered from guilt when they saw young people being arrested, while they could not do anything to help them. Yet others felt guilty when they witnessed their fellow protesters being arrested, and then had to go into exile while they themselves escaped to safety. As they described it, they went through an emotional roller-coaster, all the time interrogating themselves on how they could do better, and taking themselves out to the street, regardless of the consequences.

Positive emotions referred to the heartfelt experiences of mutual help and encouragement in the Movement. Not only did these experiences strengthen the trust in their comrades, but this trust, added to their faith and feelings for Hong Kong, greatly enhanced the solidarity and loyalty to the Movement. Many of our interviewees were able to recount moving personal episodes and stories: some received continuous backup and other support; some had unforgettable memories of mutual help and silent rapport with fellow protesters; yet others were deeply grateful for the company and generous support from others. Sacrifices made without consideration for reward, support rendered regardless of danger, and strenuous input into the Movement: all these, apart from furnishing numerous unforgettable clips of memories, also brought home to the interviewees the solidarity and incredibly firm resolve of the Hongkongers. Even when they did not know one another, people could still coordinate their efforts for a shared goal. When there was good will, people from different backgrounds and generations could indeed cooperate well. Though their encounters were fortuitous and brief, the participants of the Movement were closely interconnected through an imperceptible but strong sense of solidarity. Together, they formed a community with a common stand and shared worries. The term "Hongkonger" (香港人), pronounced *hoeng-gong-jan* in Cantonese, now comes to signify not merely residents of a region, but members of a comradely community.

4   Lest We Forget

Our study took place in the second half of 2019 when the Anti-ELAB Movement was at its height. With the surge of the COVID-19 pandemic in early 2020, and the National Security Law (Hong Kong) being passed in mid-year, this Movement, which had raged locally and even impacted international politics, now died down. Today is the time when Beijing and the powerholders in Hong Kong purge and take revenge on those who dare to oppose them. Years 2021–2022 see daily court cases conducted at various levels, with the defendants being young people accused of "riot", as well as middle-aged and elderly persons – veterans of the democracy movement – accused of "inciting unlawful assembly", many of whom were remanded in custody, convicted, or sentenced. The Department of Justice not only "revitalises" laws that were passed in the old colonial days but are long taken by the international legal community as violating human rights,[5] but it also creates new "crimes" under the National Security Law (Hong Kong). For example, in early 2021, 55 people who had either organised or participated in the primary election (for the Legislative Council elections) for the pro-democracy camp in 2020 were arrested for "inciting subversion of state power". Among them, 47 were rejected bail and were remanded in custody on 28th February 2021. This set the record of the highest number of arrestees, in the same case, being remanded without trial.[6] Up to the end of 2020, more than 10,000 people had been arrested for their involvement in the Anti-Extradition Movement. This number, plus the new "crimes" arising from the National Security Law, pushed the Hong Kong prison population to a ten-year high.[7]

Looking back, the Anti-Extradition Movement in 2019 was the prelude to the demise of the political institution, culture, and values of Hong Kong. Severe political repression also triggered a new wave of emigration or flight from the territory.[8] Detailed discussion of this will be made in Chap. 13. Suffice it to note

---

5   The Public Order Ordinance, which prohibits "unlawful assembly", was passed in the aftermath of the 1967 riots, in November of that year. Following the enactment of the Hong Kong Bill of Rights in 1991, most provisions in the law were repealed in the Legislative Council in 1995. However, in February 1997, the Standing Committee of the National People's Congress passed a resolution that these amendments to the Public Order Ordinance would be scrapped.

6   Forty-seven of the 55 arrested were charged, and out of these, only 13 of them were released on bail subsequently up to the time of writing (September 2022). See "[47 preliminary election case] Pang Cheuk-kei applied successfully for change in conditions for bail", *inmediahk. net*, 5 Aug 2022, (in Chinese) https://tinyurl.com/2sz89fyr (last viewed 13 Sept 2022).

7   See the following quote: "It should be noted that as the legal proceedings of the cases in relation to the social disturbances were in progress, there was an increase in the number of remands. The average daily number of remands hit a decade high last year, from 1436 in 2011 to 1962 in 2020, representing an increase of 37 per cent. The highest single-day number of remands in 2020 stood at 2195, representing an increase of 613 persons (39 per cent) when compared with the corresponding figure (1582 persons) in 2011. The department expects that the relevant figures will remain high and have a further upward trend this year", from "Correctional Services Department 2020's Annual Review", The Government of the Hong Kong SAR Press Releases, 23 April 2021. https://www.info.gov.hk/gia/general/202104/28/P20 21042800357.htm?fontSize=1 (last viewed 13 Sept 2022).

8   See, for example, "4 out of 10 Hongkongers would emigrate if given the opportunity – survey", *Hong Kong Free Press*, 8 Oct 2020. https://hongkongfp.com/2020/10/08/4-out-of-10-hong

here that, paradoxically, a new "community of protest" (Ma, 2020) has emerged amidst this demise, as the identity and values of Hongkongers undergo a process of redefinition and reintegration. We do not know what would come out of this interplay between demise and reintegration: there are numerous factors shaping Hong Kong's fate after all. Yet, we believe that it is always important to make historical records of what has happened, no matter what or how changes would come about. The voices of 56 persons who had participated in the 2019 Anti-Extradition Movement are hereby recorded for future times. In Part Two, we present the stories of five of our interviewees. Through these stories, we hope to convey the intentions, views, and emotions behind the actions of some of the participants in greater detail and depth.

---

kongers-would-emigrate-if-given-the-opportunity-survey/ (Report on telephone survey conducted by the Institute of Asia-Pacific Studies, The Chinese University of Hong Kong, last viewed 13 Sept 2022).

PART 2

The Stories

∴

CHAPTER 8

Brick, a University Graduate: "Since Then, the Fights Defined Me"

Brick is a university graduate in her early 20s. When she was in secondary school, she participated in a June 4th gathering and a July 1st rally with her senior school fellows for the first time. In 2014, the young woman slept out in the open on Harcourt Road in Admiralty during the Umbrella Revolution. Five years later, she had her fair share of experience with tear gas on the streets.

Before the Anti-ELAB Movement broke out, Brick had started to pay attention to the development when the government announced a draft amendment to the Fugitive Offenders Ordinance. To her, the "Co-location Arrangement"[1] that was passed earlier, which contravened the "One Country, Two Systems" arrangement, was like a boulder hitting the lake, yet there was no ripple. "I wasn't in Hong Kong at that time, but I looked at it and thought: Wow, why didn't anything happen? Why was there no response from anyone? I knew from the beginning of the Anti-ELAB Movement that there would be another bill of that sort, and I also predicted that it would pass in a similar way." In March 2019, she had already participated in the rally organised by the Civil Human Rights Front, but participation was not that high, with only about 10,000 participants at the peak.

> Before you are raped, shout out at the top of your voice, no matter what ... After the Umbrella Revolution, I participated in all the social movements in that frame of mind. I knew it wouldn't achieve anything, I knew there wouldn't be enough people participating, but I still had to go out and take part.

---

1 After heated debate in the Legislative Council, the "co-location arrangement" was implemented in the West Kowloon Terminus, the last station of the Guangzhou-Shenzhen-Hong Kong Railway, in September 2018, despite strong opposition from pro-democracy legislators. In practice, mainland Chinese customs officers are allowed to set up their checkpoints and exercise their jurisdiction in the West Kowloon Terminus, which is technically situated in the Hong Kong Special Administrative Region. This was seen by the opponents as a contravention of the "One Country, Two Systems" arrangement principle guaranteed by the Sino-British Joint Declaration and the Basic Law.

Brick was still a teenager at the time of the 2014 Umbrella Revolution. Out of her passion for reporting, she interviewed participants and wrote reports in the occupied area in Admiralty. Yet, she was not very involved in the Movement at that time. "I was a bit of a twit; I merely went there to sleep, so naturally I made very little contribution." Five years later, in the early morning of June 12, 2019, demonstrators occupied Harcourt Road in Admiralty again. This time, Brick's goal was clear. "I recognised the members of the Legislative Council; the purpose was to prevent the passage of the bill, so we had to stop them and prevent them from going to work." The training she had in writing her thesis gave her an advantage over other protesters, enabling her to clearly identify the pro-establishment members of the Legislative Council. Her primary duty that day was to keep watch and guard the entrance and exit of the Legislative Council Building.

Later, the conflict between the police and the demonstrators heated up, and the first rubber bullet was fired under the Bo-dai.[2] Faced with more than 100 heavily armed police officers, Brick and other demonstrators had to retreat. Because the police blocked the roads, they got trapped near the AIA Carnival booths. "Those fences were two to three metres high, and we were stuck there. We couldn't get out at all, but the police kept firing tear gas, trying to arrest all of us." With nowhere to go, a large group of demonstrators frantically pushed down the boarding, rushed into the nearby carnival ground, and then rushed to the waterfront, but the police were relentless. "They continued to chase the demonstrators, even inside the shopping mall. There were undercover detectives there; they must have been waiting in the toilets."

For Brick, June 12 was a turning point, which saw the illusion of *"wo lei fei"*[3] completely shattered. "At that time, you still had the illusion that since we so easily occupied both sides, we could hang in there, maybe for a few days, and we could drag it out. Yet, in just one afternoon, one second, ... suddenly, you realised the imbalance of power between the two sides, and the fact that they [could have but] didn't stop you right at the beginning of the Umbrella Revolution [in 2014]." Facing the force of batons, tear gas, bean-bag bullets, etc., she believed that peaceful marches had lost their effect, and the only way was to arm oneself, and at the same time to adopt a host of multiple

---

2 *Bo-dai*, literally "under the pot". "Under the pot" refers to the area below the cylindrical structure of the Legislative Council Complex, inside of which is the main chamber. This area outside and underneath the chamber used to be the designated protest area. Since the structure resembles a rice pot, this area was usually referred to by the protesters as *Bo-dai*.

3 *Wo lei fei*, in Cantonese, literally "peaceful, rational, and non-violent", refers to those protesters who insisted on using peaceful, non-violent means. This is referred to as PRN in Part One.

means of resistance, including winning the support of other countries and the "International Front" in sanctioning China and Hong Kong.

In mid-July of the same year, Brick was arrested for the first time, not on the front lines of the conflict, but at a rally where a Letter of No Objection had been issued. Despite having given prior approval, the police suddenly rushed into the meeting place. "I told my friends, like those principled Ls:[4] it's mad. It [the notice] is still valid, I'm here, what do they arrest me for?" The fact was that the police still arrested me. "At that time, I still had some illusion, and felt that the arrest under that circumstance was not legal. Later, I found out that it didn't matter to the police. One could be arrested for illegal gathering even if one was just strolling about and happened to be near a site of demonstration."

Due to political disagreement with her family, after her arrest, Brick had to lie about a friend having just broken up with her boyfriend, and that she was going to keep her friend company and therefore was not going home that night. However, she didn't go to work the next morning, and her mobile phone was turned off. Because her "broken-hearted" friend had also been arrested, her family was unable to contact her. During that time, there was a claim of "wave of suicides" in the community, and many people were expressing the desire to commit suicide on social platforms. "I often quarrelled with my family at home, and sometimes they made very nasty comments ... and I felt very down and dejected. My family was worried and wondered whether my friend and I would be so stupid as to contemplate killing ourselves."

The family finally found out the truth. Since then, her family had been very nervous about her whereabouts. Brick's bag was once searched by her mother when she went out. "But that time, I really didn't go to demonstrate. I just happened to be in Causeway Bay to watch a documentary, and it happened that there were some actions that night." Her mother took two weeks' leave from work and stayed home to guard over her. Brick could only turn to the online platform temporarily to continue the fight. "She saw that and told me off. I said, 'you wouldn't let me out, so I stay in. Isn't that okay with you?'"

In August, she returned to the streets, which, by that time, was full of tear gas. She was mainly responsible for supplies, sentinels, rear guard, transportation, etc. However, she revealed that she had been on "the very first row on the front line", but after being arrested, she did not dare go too much to

---

4   "L", an acronym for the Cantonese swear-word "Lun". When used after an adjective, it means, derogatively, a person has a very strong quality designated by that adjective. "Principled L" refers to someone who is *very* principled, i.e., too principled.

the front. She admitted that she became most lost in August. After the occupation of the Legislative Council on July 1, everything was chaotic and there was polarisation among the protesters. "[I] was on my last legs, but if I could, I would continue to go out, to have a try. Even if I couldn't achieve anything, I wanted people around me to know that I would come, that I wasn't going home to rest."

"Later it became more miserable. After October 1, friends came out less frequently." On October 1, the National Day of the People's Republic of China, demonstrators clashed violently with the police in various districts. One of them, Tsang Chi-kin, a Form 5 (Year 11) student, was shot in the chest by a policeman at close range with live ammunition.[5] The police arrested a total of 269 people that day, including 178 men and 91 women, aged between 12 and 71.

> In the past, when someone asked in the [chat]group if anyone wanted to go out, many people responded. Later, maybe because there were too many activities, some people started to feel tired or lazy, and it became a bit embarrassing to ask this question, so we no longer asked in the group. We would discuss via private messages, and the size was no longer ... There used to be a lot of people, a group of maybe seven people, [but] now only a few of us would arrange to go out.

In mid-November, the university campuses became battlefields, with the worst ones at the Chinese University of Hong Kong (CUHK) and the Hong Kong Polytechnic University (PolyU). Looking back now, Brick thinks it was irrational to insist on remaining at the campuses. "I believe that unless it was the Legislative Council or the Chief Executive's Office, and staying put there would stop their operation, there was no point in staying. We could have simply gone back the next day to block access." However, as a CUHK alumna, even though there was no more public transport that night, she still went to the nearest location by bus, and then took a long walk to the campus. "I could understand

---

5   Despite his serious injuries, the 18-year-old Tsang Chi-kin recovered, but was arrested for assault on police and rioting. He did not turn up in court in December 2020, and it was rumoured that he had left Hong Kong. However, the police re-arrested him on 14 July 2022, and he was remanded at the time of writing. See "Shot during the Anti-ELAB Movement in Tsuen Wan in 2019, Tsang Chi-kin arrested by Regional Crime Unit, Will appear in court on Thursday", *HK01*, (in Chinese), 14 July 2022. https://tinyurl.com/bda4rwbh (last viewed 13 Sept 2022).

why we protesters wanted to stay put. It was not a rational decision; it came from a totally irrational state of mind."

> When it came to the PolyU, I respected the decision of those inside on whether to stay or not. I believe there was also a group of students who felt the same way as us, the CUHK alumni.

Compared to the CUHK, the situation at the PolyU was even more desperate. Hundreds of demonstrators were trapped in the campus, heavily surrounded by riot police. Some people tried to escape by abseiling, some crawled out through the sewers. Other demonstrators tried to "surround Wei and save Zhao"[6] by tackling the police along the roads near PolyU, but to no avail. Brick knew very well that against the number, the deployment, and the force of the police, there was no chance for them to succeed.

> It was impossible to break through, they would simply be going along Nathan Road symbolically ... It was just a symbolic action, to tell the people inside that 'we have not abandoned you'.

Brick recalled that at the time, she heard someone shouting: "We need to disperse. If those in the back don't go, those in the front can't go." Later, she learnt that the police had fired a lot of tear gas in the Yaumatei area, and demonstrators ran in all directions to try and escape, and this almost resulted in a fatal stampede. "So, it's not worth it in the end, but we had to do it ... It's the same for the whole movement. Rationally, a lot of things were not worth doing, but people continued to do them."

Brick used to be a "*wo lei fei*" and once believed in the "love and peace" concept of the Umbrella Revolution. Until pan-democratic lawmakers such as Cheung Chiu Hung and Kwok Ka Kei prevented the Umbrella Movement protesters from storming the Legislative Council, and after the protesters' actions were criticised by public opinion, she began to question this "non-violent" stance. "It was just the breaking of some glass panels." She now thinks that when a movement became stagnant, the demonstrators had to "push forward", to seek more leverage against the regime. Quoting the march of a million people on June 9, she explained: "You boasted about the number, but it's not

---

6   This term connotes a strategy which involves trying to distract the enemy's attention instead of fighting head-on against a powerful and concentrated force. *Wei* and *Zhao* were two states in the Warring States period in Chinese history.

enough as a bargaining chip. You could only take the occupation route. What else could you do?"

She also agreed that demonstrators should be able to use force as a means of self-protection. "You [the police] were fully armed, my goodness! I was just throwing bricks and 'fire demons' [petrol bombs] ... You rushed over at the PolyU with a tank, against those having just those [trivial] weapons like umbrellas, petrol bombs, etc. I think [using] defensive weapons is acceptable."

In the later stage of the movement, violent incidents done "in private" became more and more frequent. Some protesters ganged up and attacked people who supported the government, and someone targeted a police officer by knifing his neck. Brick said that these actions were excessive, and believed that when protesters used force, they should not cause serious injury or put people's lives in danger. "For example, setting fire to that elderly gentleman was unnecessary;[7] using a drainage cover to attack someone trying to clear the roadblocks was similarly unnecessary. He [the attacked] had his rights, too."

Brick once saw someone on Telegram initiating a vote which asked: If you only need to press a button, and "bang!", the entire police force would be killed, would you choose to press the button? In the end, 70 to 80 per cent of the respondents indicated that they would choose to press the button, but Brick still believes that the bottom line of using force is "I don't want you to die."

She initially tried to post online, for example, advising demonstrators to keep clear of lifts and traffic lights when "refurbishing"[8] to avoid endangering some users such as the elderly and children. The online responses were polarised, with some agreeing and others being sarcastic. However, as the conflict continued to heat up, she no longer believed that online debates could stop behaviour that went beyond acceptable boundaries. "If I was on the scene, I could catch them and tell them off; otherwise, I could only post on Facebook. They swiped the screen, saw my messages, and just thought I was being silly. There was no way I could convince them unless I could talk to them face to face."

When asked about the division of labour between men and women during the movement, Brick said frankly that there was an advantage for men to be

---

7   A 57-year-old man was set on fire by someone dressed in black, after having quarrelled with protesters in a metro station on 11 November 2019. He suffered from serious burn injuries. The perpetuator(s) disappeared and could not be found, allegedly having left Hong Kong. See "Ma-On-Shan man on fire. The arsonist and accomplice left territory. Two men arrested for buying plane tickets on their behalf", *HK01*, 15 Jan 2021, https://tinyurl.com/4pa93d5k (in Chinese, last viewed 14 Sept 2022).

8   "*Refurbishing*" is a euphemism for vandalising public facilities or premises of businesses that are considered pro-government or pro-Beijing.

responsible for work that required strength, but she and other women tried their utmost to not use gender stereotypes to divide up the duties. "Now there are talks of only marrying the frontline *bas*' or 'rear services *sis*'.[9] I wonder why that is. What is the reason for sisters only responsible for rear services? Why can't brothers do that? Why can't sisters go to the front line?" Among her friends, there were boys doing publicity materials and girls going to the front lines.

A scholar once severely criticised the movement's "patriarchy". As a girl, Brick felt that there was no difference in the right of men and women to speak in the movement, as far as her personal experience was concerned. "My male friends did not discriminate against women. At the most they felt you were useless [in frontline conflicts], and they had to protect a friend, so they said, 'stand back a little', or 'wear something [to protect yourself]', but there was no gender discrimination." She also explained that the reason for her working on backup services was purely because she was not physically strong enough. She added: "Many frontline girls were really fantastic."

When it comes to the participation of university students in the movement, Brick sums it up like this: "I am very subjective and as a matter of course feel very proud of the CUHK alumni taking a strong stance at the university." She believes that the education at CUHK has shaped a group of idealists. "They would feel that 'This is what I should do'. Everyone had the basic visions drawn from certain schools of political philosophy, and everyone took it very seriously to learn and to discuss. I had asked friends from the University of Hong Kong and from other universities. No one would be as silly as to go to attend classical political philosophy seminars after class, and then discuss it together." She said that most CUHK alumni might not have gone to the forefront, but they were deeply involved in many different ways, such as the "International Front": "not just in the publicity materials, or on Twitter, but in the more practical and also visionary things."

However, Brick also agrees that people from the university or the middle-class were generally more protective of themselves and might not necessarily fight on the front lines on the streets. She bluntly said that her family's expectations of her had also become shackles. "Every day I was condemning myself for not achieving the ideals that I pursued, not doing my best, and then I was pulled back by external factors such as my family. I struggled with this every

---

9   "*Ba*" means brother, and "*si*", sister. Participants in the Anti-ELAB Movement normally referred to one another as brothers or sisters if they wanted to distinguish the gender. Otherwise, they used the gender-neutral term of "*sau zuk*", literally meaning "hands and feet", a long-used Chinese expression for siblings.

day." She believes that no matter how far at the front you stood in this movement, you would never feel that you had done enough, so long as you cared.
"Everyone is burdened by a sense of guilt."

> I read media reports that, after having climbed out from the drainage [the
> sewers] for more than ten hours, a young [PolyU] student climbed back
> in to save people. I thought to myself, wow, how much have they [already]
> done? However, in the report, he felt that he had not done enough, oth-
> erwise why would he climb back in after more than ten hours? Anyone in
> any position had that mentality.

Brick admits that she lives in guilt every day, as do her friends who have had
similar experiences. "I cry when I come across a poster on the streets, you
would cry when you think about it. My friends are the same; we always feel we
haven't done enough."

> There's nothing we could do. Just wait for it [the Chinese Communist
> Party] to perish. Only when it is weak will we have room to live. Hong
> Kong has always been in such a crevice. When the economy was down,
> it [Mainland China] depended on you. Now that the economy is up it
> doesn't think you have any worth ... I don't know. It has always been said
> that we have to wait for its collapse, we have to gradually build ourselves
> up. It could be independence, or a federal system, that's also possible. It
> doesn't have to be independence, but we will only be able to see it when
> it collapses.

In Brick's eyes, the democratic movement used to be slow and gradual, but
now her generation hopes to use stronger and even more radical means to gain
more political leverage. "People no longer just go on marches or raise placards;
they choose to go on strike at the universities ... You must keep pushing with
these issues, and if it comes to a standstill, you have to ask: What to do now,
give up again? Is that it?"

Brick says that she feels restless every day and is eager to see change. Every
day she asks herself, "Hey, what have you done today?" Under the unjust system, she just wants to do her best to resist. "We won't die, and we can still
make a living. If the economy collapses, we will continue to play this game (of
making a living), but I just think this game is unfair. From the very beginning,
why should I be the one to pay the mortgage? Why can't you be the one to pay
for the property? Why should I be so miserable? Just because you made the
rules, right?"

Brick clearly states that what her generation pursues is a subject consciousness for Hong Kong people. "Economic success cannot define us, at least not for this generation. What we pursue is not material things." This pursuit leads to a series of philosophical questions: Who are we? Why do we have to survive here? What is our culture? Brick is convinced that only by continuing to ask questions and trying to answer those questions can we establish the subject consciousness of Hong Kong people.

Brick believes that to build up a sense of subject consciousness, Hong Kong people must "export" revolution to China. She mentions that in many marches in the past, people deliberately shouted slogans in Putonghua, especially when they walked past hotels, where mainland tourists stayed. She explains that the establishment of subject consciousness requires not only verbal affirmation, but also practice and action. "Every time I went on the march, it was as if I was telling myself about the differences between me and them, and why I had to resist, and that defined me."

Brick had considered going abroad after graduation, but when the anti-extradition movement erupted, she temporarily put aside her plans. She didn't start looking for a part-time job until a few weeks before. Now, she is still struggling about leaving Hong Kong. "I want to stay, and I don't want to stay. I don't want to stay because of myself and my family. There is too much tension at home every day."

Brick said that her mother secretly understood her daughter's thoughts, but because her husband was "very blue" (i.e., pro-establishment), she had to take sides. "She was facing the two of us [Brick and her father] and she was torn between us, resulting nearly in a split personality, so she chose the 'blue' side. I want to leave, but I also want to stay in Hong Kong. If this is not the case at my home, I will fight tooth and nail with you. What does it matter? If I don't go abroad, I will 'break stones'[10] here and do community work."

> You couldn't define what Hong Kong people were during the Umbrella Revolution, and I couldn't answer that myself. When people said, 'Oh, because I love Hong Kong so much, I come out', I asked myself, 'Really? Love Hong Kong? What do I love about Hong Kong? Do I love the economic prosperity, the convenient transport, the dense population?' No, I couldn't answer that. Until the Fish Ball Revolution (riots in Mongkok in 2016), I began to realise that the characteristic of our generation was that

---

10   "Break stones" is a colloquial expression in Cantonese, which refers to the tedious work of breaking stones into small chips, taking small steps and doing seemingly trivial, but ground-laying work.

we wanted to define ourselves. To define ourselves is to pursue certain values. Perhaps we all have some persistence in our character, perhaps at least we feel those are important issues. Our opinions about them are a separate thing; at least we've paid attention to these issues, and that has already made a difference.

CHAPTER 9

Streambreaker at Seventeen: "If You Ask Me What Has Been Sacrificed ... It's Probably My Future"

He is 17 this year, a secondary school boy. He loves philosophy and avidly reads books on civil rights. "I quite buy into the ideology of Malcom X, the African-American leader in the civil rights movement," he says and then continues to talk keenly about the entry grades required by various local universities like the Chinese University, Hong Kong University, and Lingnan University for their undergraduate programmes in Philosophy, as keenly as when one is enumerating a valuable family collection. Whilst he treasures the hope to read Philosophy in college, he also desires to be an actor. "I am a member of the Drama Club in school." Alas, all the dreams and passions he shares are invariably appended with "if I had not been charged ..." This is the predicament faced by our young people in present-day Hong Kong.

He calls himself 'Streambreaker'. He was a Form 5 (Year 11) secondary school student when he participated in his first-ever protest march on June 9, 2019. It was organised by the Civil Human Rights Front. This march was a peaceful protest against the controversial Extradition (Amendment) Bill. Participants were recommended to wear white as a symbol of justice and this turned out to be the only occasion in the whole movement that this colour was recommended. Thereafter, only seas of black were seen in rallies. "I have been using IG (Instagram), and there's a lot of information about this upcoming march on June 9. In school, the Liberal Studies teacher talked about this extradition bill and how a murder suspect, Chan Tung-Kai, came into the picture. So, I know what's going on." Streambreaker recounts.

Streambreaker joined the June 9 demonstration alone. "It was a spur-of-the-moment decision." But after having taken part in it, he started to think differently.

> There was then an on-line signature drive to rally people's support to have the proposed Amendment Bill scrapped. Apparently around 700,000 to 800,000 signatures were gathered. But I felt that street protests should be more effective than signature-collecting. I was hoping instead of merely providing their signatures, there would be more people taking to the

streets. What happened subsequently would indeed have a most encouraging impact if it had not been for Carrie Lam.

The Civil Human Rights Front announced that one million participants were estimated to have taken part in the June 9 demonstration. Despite this huge turn-out, Chief Executive Carrie Lam still decided to press ahead with the scheduled second reading debate of the extradition amendment bill in the Legislative Council on June 12.

> I was not keen on politics before this proposed amendment bill. Of course, I was aware that there had been a rally in which demonstrators protested against the West Kowloon High-speed Rail Joint Checkpoint Bill and that such noises just fell on the government's deaf ears. The bill was passed, nonetheless. This time massive discontent with the bill has clearly been demonstrated, with the size of one million demonstrators on June 9. Yet the government still ignored our views. It was totally unacceptable.

Streambreaker admits that he "was greatly dissatisfied" and "was prompted all the more to take part in the protest on June 12, the day of the second reading debate in LegCo". On that day, there was a class-boycott activity at school in which he participated. When school was over, he casually took a collapsible umbrella, donned a surgical mask, and hurried to Admiralty where the LegCo building was. "I wasn't thinking consciously then that I needed the umbrella for self-defence. I just took it without much thinking. When I arrived at Admiralty, it was already 5 or 6 in the evening."

All the way on the metro from school to Admiralty, Streambreaker was watching live feeds on the protests on his mobile. "I watched how the police deployed tear gas at the protesters. When I knew somebody got shot in the eye, I was very emotional and wanted to be at the scene immediately." When he finally arrived at Admiralty MTR station, he found that most of its exits were already closed. As he was not familiar with the layout of the station, he started talking to a stranger who had been tear-gassed and was told the route to escape from the police's encirclement. Streambreaker says before he took part in the one million people's rally on June 9, he had approached some of his classmates to see if anyone was going with him. But nobody was. So, if nobody had joined him for the peaceful rally on June 9, it would have been futile to approach them again for this one on June 12.

When Streambreaker emerged from the Admiralty MTR station, dusk had fallen, and the sky was darkening. He turned left after walking through a shopping mall and he caught sight of one of the 'protesters supply stations'. He could see that the protesters had already 'occupied' the road by tying the police's crowd control barriers together to form a barricade. When he approached the barricade from the side of the road, he saw that the riot police had already spread themselves out in a line opposite. "I then walked up to join the protesters standing in front of this defence line. I was thinking that my presence might add to their number and bolster the defence." Standing alongside him were all young people. There he stood fearlessly with them until the MTR announced that the last train for the day would pull out of the station soon. He then ran quickly back to the Admiralty MTR Station and took the last train out of Admiralty with some other protesters.

June 9 and June 12 were followed by another important date, June 15. There was to be another organised mass rally on June 16 by the Civil Human Rights Front. However, in the afternoon of June 15, the Chief Executive announced a 'temporary suspension' of the Extradition Bill and also claimed that she would communicate with the community. That same night on June 15, a young protester, Leung Ling-kit, fell to his death from Pacific Place in Admiralty. The Civil Human Rights Front decided to go ahead with the planned June 16 demonstration for it believed that 'temporary suspension' was not the same as withdrawing the bill. The mass rally on June 16 was the second one organised by the Civil Human Rights Front. Even though there was a heavy downpour, there was a massive turnout of two million participants. "Casualties were reported in this rally, and I felt really bad. I was expecting the turnout to be under one million, but we ended up having two million. It was really astounding." Streambreaker recounts.

Streambreaker admits that on this June 16 march, he 'cursed aloud' at the police that he saw along the way. "They didn't react. They didn't beat us. It seemed just sheer indifference." But such a stance of the police did not last long. Soon, it was history. The confrontation mode between the police and the protesters changed. Should one curse at the police, one would easily be charged with assault, or worse, riot.

June 16 has not deterred Streambreaker, this secondary student, from taking to the street. On July 1, the LegCo Chamber was briefly occupied by the protesters. "When I saw news of them storming the LegCo building, I was preoccupied with my own things. Night had fallen when I finally rushed to LegCo in Admiralty." He and some protesters helped transport bricks for the roadblock. Soon it was after 10 pm. He then walked into the LegCo building and walked around inside. He was thinking to himself that at least he had seen the place. Streambreaker was not scared then. When he saw that the occupiers were not doing much inside the LegCo building, he instead felt quite safe. Meanwhile he kept reminding himself that he had to leave before the last MTR train pulled out of the station. It was only when he watched the live stream of what was happening inside the occupied building that he realised some protesters decided to retreat from it. "If I had been arrested then, it was not worth it, for my entering the LegCo wasn't really to show my approval of this act. Not that I was against it, I was merely thinking of not to 'cut the mat'[1] with these frontliners even though I didn't quite understand the purpose of occupying the LegCo chamber."

Streambreaker has been adopting a rational and peaceful attitude when he took part in the Anti-ELAB Movement. He reckons it was his experience in the 'Reclaiming Sheung Shui' protest on July 13 that changed his approach. "It was this protest that I evolved from a peaceful protester to a 'valiant' one." On that day, he found the protesters getting agitated. It seemed natural for him to take on the role of trying to calm everyone down. Suddenly some protesters sensed that something was not right with the situation and started running for their lives. Without thinking, Streambreaker followed and took to his feet as well. However, a plump boy fell right onto Streambreaker's legs. Amid chaos, some people tried to pull the plump boy up. On failing to do so, they just fled as the situation was critical. Streambreaker managed to pick himself up. He then tried to hoist the plump boy from the ground as well. It was not easy. At this moment, the riot police with long shields overtook him from behind. He was taken aback by this and let go of the boy. He then sprinted as hard as he could to escape from the scene. Even though he was pepper-sprayed from behind and was hit by a long shield on his back, he kept running. "Luckily, I wasn't arrested."

Streambreaker continues, "As my back had been injured before, it was quite sore after I was hit by the police's long shield. Also, the pepper spray was very irritating to the skin. Luckily a thirtyish man propped me up and we were able to walk to the bus stop. At the bus stop, the man washed my eyes with saline solution. There were other men around. They stayed and chatted with each other a bit." This experience ricocheted for Streambreaker.

> The riot police pepper-sprayed me ferociously. Even though it was from the back, my eyes were badly affected. I also thought that it was unnecessary for them to hit me with the long shield. The focus of the movement began to shift from 'removing altogether' the 'Extradition Bill' to

---

1   A popular term used during the 2019 protests. This came from an ancient Chinese story, when two good friends went separate ways, and this was symbolised by their cutting up the mat which they had shared to sit on in the study room into two.

'police brutality'. My personal experience has impacted a change in my bottom line.

Streambreaker frankly admits that before his July 13 experience, he would try to stop protesters from cutting off bicycle chains which would be used for tying water-filled barriers together as roadblocks. He said he was looking at it from a moral point of view and reckoned that it was improper to tamper with personal belongings. But soon after July 13, he would not stop protesters from doing such things. "I'll accommodate their behaviour even though I still cannot bring myself to do it. I simply would not cause damage to other people's personal belongings. At least I have never attempted to do it."

The morning after July 13, somebody organised an anti-extradition mass rally in Sha Tin. This rally unexpectedly received a "no-objection letter" from the police. Streambreaker would have preferred to take part in a protest which was nearer home if it had not been for what happened on July 13. He decided that as long as there were rallies, he would take part in them all to the best of his capacity. On July 14, Streambreaker behaved more daringly. He joined the protesters in roadblocks for the first time. "In the beginning, it was rather peaceful. Later the police started using pepper spray and the situation became chaotic ... Some protesters started forming human chains to transport defence gear. As for me, I helped with tying the water-filled barriers together."

Streambreaker himself was 'geared up' with what total strangers had given him in earlier demonstration scenes: helmet, goggles, face mask, and an umbrella. Across from them, the police were organising their tactical line. Streambreaker and the other protesters on the other side were either standing or sitting on the ground. Between them and the police were some pan-democracy legislative councillors who were beseeching both sides to stay calm. "They were mocked by some protesters who said that they hadn't been doing much in the past 20 years ... Meanwhile I was walking around either helping with tying the barriers together or rendering assistance of other nature."

Streambreaker had a 'shield' made of hard cardboard paper and empty plastic bottles. "I thought it might be useful and so was holding it in one hand. And in the other, I was holding an umbrella. I resisted throwing bricks at the police. I didn't throw any." At around 7 or 8 pm, the police started advancing towards the protesters and the latter slowly backed away. "At that time, nobody was thinking of confronting the police head-on. There was no such mentality then."

Somebody then shouted that they should rush towards the police. This might break up their formation line and the protesters would have an escape route. However, Streambreaker did not think it was possible. "The police were all carrying shields and pepper spray. It was not possible to break up their formation.

So, I tried to persuade my fellow protesters to use other peaceful means and hoped that the police would let us go." But Streambreaker was scoffed at by other protesters for making such a suggestion. Everyone was inclined to rush forward to break up the encirclement. But as soon as they made some slight movements, the police immediately moved closer towards them. "Finally, we simply told the police that we only wanted to leave, that we would not take any action. Still, they closed in ...".

Some protesters started to turn around and run. Streambreaker joined them. "Since I ran faster than the others, I helped to block the on-coming traffic for the others to make their way across the road. Actually, I had no idea which direction we should run for our safety. I just kept dashing forward." Finally, Streambreaker followed those who knew the way and arrived at Tai Wai MTR Station. They then went their own way from there. "As I still had to go to school the following day, I headed home. It was only when I watched the news later that I knew a policeman had his finger bitten off by a protester." The confrontations between the police and the protesters in Sha Tin lasted till five or six in the evening and they were turbulent. A team of riot police rushed into the New Town Mall and the MTR announced that trains would not stop at Sha Tin Station ... . Looking back, Streambreaker says, "I was very scared that I would be caught that day. Luckily it didn't happen."

Since that day, no matter when and where, as long as there were rallies, Streambreaker would take part. On July 21, the Civil Human Rights Front organised its sixth anti-extradition march. Its original planned route was to march from Victoria Park in Causeway Bay to Luard Road in Wanchai. However, the demonstrators changed the end point to the Liaison Office of the Central People's Government in the Western District. "When I was in Sheung Wan, I already saw the police firing a lot of rubber bullets and tear gas. I was very scared because I had been pepper-sprayed before and had a serious allergic reaction." Fearing that he might slow down the front line, Streambreaker chose not to station at the very front of it. "Armed with our home-made shields, we slowly retreated until we reached the chain eatery, Yoshinoya. We also threw eggs at the police." Streambreaker stayed at the scene until very late. By then the MTR trains had stopped running. Eventually he was given a lift home by a social worker whom he met at the scene. "We didn't exchange contact numbers. But the mutual concern and understanding was heartfelt."

The impetus of the 'white T-shirts' incident that took place at night on July 21 in Yuen Long MTR Station led to an 'anti-triad' and 'anti-police violence' demonstration on July 27. As approval for this demonstration was not granted by the authority, a lot of citizens resorted to 'window-shopping' on the streets of Yuen Long. Streambreaker was there as well. The anger that he harboured after what happened to him on July 21 led him to stronger 'valiant' behaviour. When the police fired rubber bullets at the protesters, Streambreaker rushed forward with his shield to fend them off and threw water bottles at the police. "Somebody has brought along some home-made American Captain style metal shields. Picking up one of them and using it to protect my head and body, I rushed towards the police. Unfortunately, I was hit in the leg by a bullet and collapsed after a few steps."

Streambreaker's leg was hit by a sponge grenade. Still, he managed to get away with the help of some protesters. They took him to a hospital. At the hospital, he dared not reveal anything. When asked for his ID card, he claimed that it was lost. He also gave himself a false name. "I just said that I fell while playing football. The hospital gave me an x-ray to ensure that there was no fracture and then bandaged the wound for me." It was obvious that the wound was a bullet-induced one, and Streambreaker knew that the doctor and nurses did not really believe what he said about sustaining injury from a fall. He continued after a pause, "at one point the doctor asked me who was at the scene of my injury, black dogs (bad police) or white dogs (triads)? I simply told him I saw just the black ones, not the whites."

Streambreaker was a loner in all these demonstrations. It was very rare for him to take the initiative to acquaint himself with other protesters. There was only this one time that he exchanged contact numbers with an 'elder sister' (a female 'sau zuk'). Both attempted once to quit the movement. He also made the acquaintance of a frontliner who later became a behind-the-scenes musician in the August 18 protest. "This guy had formed a secondary student group and would occasionally organise gatherings for us. He said these activities helped to reinforce ties among us. Once he treated us to a Korean BBQ."

Streambreaker took part in many rallies and has forgotten the details of many. However, those of the Kwai Chung demonstration on August 25 would always stay. "I was arrested ... my waist and my limbs sustained many injuries from the police's beatings." It was a very long day for Streambreaker. When he set out for the demonstration, the Tsuen Wan MTR station was already closed. So he took a bus to Kwai Chung. When he arrived, he busied himself with what he normally did – helping to set up makeshift roadblocks etc. The mood was already quite tense, so he took refuge in a nearby park. But soon the riot police arrived at his refuge spot. They exchanged looks with each other and then the police raced towards him. Streambreaker spirited away and luckily, he managed to. He kept watching the news broadcast and realised that there were still many protesters guarding the demonstration scene. He wanted to locate them. As he didn't know his way, he failed to do so. Instead, he joined another group of over a hundred protesters who planned to leave Kwai Chung for other districts where similar demonstrations were taking place. They wanted to lend their support to these other protesters. It was already past 10 pm. Streambreaker took a bus to Lai Chi Kok. But then it was raining hard. He was soaked and decided to take shelter in a friend's place. However, his friend was not at home. Meanwhile he learnt from Telegram (TG) groups that the riot police were in operation in Sham Shui Po. Immediately Streambreaker changed his plan and walked all the way from Lai Chi Kok to Sham Shui Po. He joined those protesters who were demonstrating outside the Sham Shui Po Police Station. He was at the very front of the defence line shouting at the police.

He remembered a 'blue ribbon' who was present at the scene started quarrelling with the protesters. When this 'blue ribbon' eventually left the place, he left behind a pile of weapons – hiking poles, choppers, cutters, wooden poles, etc. There was a commotion among the protesters at what this 'blue ribbon' did. During the chaos, the weapons were kicked aside and were all over the place. Streambreaker spontaneously started to pick them up one by one. "All I could think of was that there was still a knife to be picked up. I was thinking that they should be gathered as evidence for the reporters. I wanted to show them the kind of weapons that this blue ribbon brought with him to the demonstration scene." It was still raining, and the scene was just chaotic. Streambreaker was bent on retrieving that knife when the riot police started arresting people. It was too late for Streambreaker to flee. No sooner was he pushed down onto the ground by the riot police then he felt himself kicked and punched all over and over. "My waist, arms and many other parts of the body were beaten. Then they tied my arms behind my back, wrenched me up from the ground, and kept using their kneecaps and feet to kick at my stomach and the lower part of my body. I was bruised all over." Streambreaker says that even though he was tied up and could not move, the riot police did not stop kicking him. When they finally finished beating him up, they threw him into the police car.

Streambreaker was bailed after being detained for over forty hours. He was charged with 'unlawful gathering'. During his detention, he could not seek the assistance of any solicitor. When the police took his statement, he only had his family with him. "My phone was confiscated. When I went home, I could only use the computer to contact friends so that they could help get me a lawyer. I then got on the TG groups to sort out my 'remaining business'. Meanwhile my mother kept shouting at me. 'Wake up! Don't be brain-washed!' she scolded. I was furious."

I then had a fierce argument with my mother, and no sooner had I returned home than I left.

When Streambreaker arrived at his friend's place, he asked for assistance to download his TG account. As soon as he located it, he contacted the musician whom he met on August 18. Streambreaker needed to urgently attend to his 'business' because he wanted to protect the other protesters. "I requested this musician acquaintance to let it be known in various 'open seas and TG groups' that I had been arrested." He also requested the musician to help contact the 612 Humanitarian Relief Fund so that I could apply for its fund to pay my bail. "The musician knew that I had run away from home, and so gave me HK$500. This kept me going for the first few days."

What then for Streambreaker? What followed his days of 'exile'? "The first night I slept in a friend's place. I had a quick bite when I got up and then there was not much to do really. The 612 Humanitarian Relief Fund 'lent' me HK$4000 as my bail money." Streambreaker felt that the lawyer who was provided by the Fund was slow in attending to his case. Therefore, he turned to Spark Alliance for assistance. As he was still a secondary student, Streambreaker knew at heart that he had to return home eventually. But he tried to procrastinate doing so and wandered here and there for some days. "I slept in MacDonald's, back-staircases, and various other places. Occasionally I went to my friends' places for showers, a fresh change of clothes and to sort out some personal affairs."

Streambreaker's mobile was kept by the police, and he had no money to buy a new one. Thus, his parents could only know his whereabouts through indirect means. "They contacted teachers at school who then called my friends to contact me. So, my parents knew that I was safe from these indirect sources. My parents tried to pass me the message that I should return home, but there were still issues that I hadn't quite worked out."

Streambreaker did not enjoy a close relationship with his parents. They seldom talked to each other. Also, their views on the protests were polemic to Streambreaker's. All these were reasons why he was reluctant to return home. To compound the problem, his arrest reminded him of some unresolved issues with his mother. Now the rift between them just widened. "When I was in junior secondary school, my mother bought me a cell phone. However, it was pre-set with a tracking function which allowed her to freely turn my phone on and read what was in it." When Streambreaker realised what his mother had done to the phone, he took it to the manufacturer to have it reset. "After knowing what I did, my mother scolded me and claimed that it was perfectly reasonable for her to monitor me. So, I reacted even more adversely." Owing to this episode, even though his mother bought him a new mobile as his was with the police, Streambreaker' mistrust of his parents caused him to "chuck the new mobile into the rubbish bin immediately. But I think she picked it up afterwards."

With no cell phone, Streambreaker could only try borrowing old ones from his friends, but most of them were in poor condition, e.g., difficulty in charging. Later the 'elder sister' mentioned earlier located him through the TG account albeit she didn't know his name. She had an old iPhone 6 for him to use.

Now that he was arrested and charged, Streambreaker knew very well that he had to be very careful in order not to be arrested again. Yet he still left his footprints in subsequent demonstrations as he had promised himself "to attend the protests in the best of his capacity". "Since I wanted to keep my promise, I set my own rules to make that work. It is like setting the number of hours I need to spend on schoolwork, and I would fulfil that goal." The night when he was arrested on August 25, he was kept in the police station until the night of August 27. But soon he was on the street again. It was August 31, the first day when the police used blue-coloured-water cannon trucks on the protesters. Streambreaker managed not to be jetted with blue water on that day even though he occasionally dared pick up canisters of tear bombs and throw them back at the police. Meanwhile his musician acquaintance managed to find him a shelter and he did not need to sleep on the street, something that he had been doing for the past few days.

At the start of the new school year, Streambreaker attempted to return home. However, he did not want to meet his parents. "When I was about to enter the building, I saw my father coming out. Immediately I turned around and went to stay at a friend's place." He only returned home the following day for a wash and change of clothes after he was certain his father was not in. Sometime in September he ended his self-imposed homeless life as he had to attend school. It was the start of a new school year and Streambreaker could not spend too much time in the Movement. September 28 was the Memorial Day for the 2014 Umbrella Movement. He said he was just a Form 1 (Year 7) student back in 2014 and had no interest in politics. But five years on in 2019, he attended its memorial event. "It took me 5 years before I started delving into what Joshua Wong said at the Umbrella Movement. After attending the memorial gathering, I followed the other attendees to protest at the police headquarters. I was standing at the very front. When somebody was hit by the blue water of the cannon trucks, I helped them to rinse the colour off."

Streambreaker took part in the anti-police protest on September 29. "It was the usual running around and being chased by the anti-riot police. I even ran up to Shue Yan University to drop off some handy resources and didn't retrieve them until October 1." On that day, Streambreaker thought of going to Admiralty. As he was worried that he would be easily arrested there, he took other means of public transport instead and went to Shue Yan University very early in the morning. After he retrieved his 'personal provision supplies', he headed towards the 'battleground' in Sha Tin. There he was taught how to be a 'fire magician' (petrol bomb making) by other protesters. "I did help a bit, but I never threw one because I didn't want to take on such a frontline position."

In the afternoon of October 4, the HKSAR government invoked a colonial emergency law banning protesters from wearing face masks. Streambreaker heard about this news at school. His school also appealed to students not to wear masks. "We ignored it of course." That same evening the MTR announced that its service for the following day would be suspended. Disregarding this inconvenience, Streambreaker donned a black mask, covered his right eye with an eye-patch and went alone to an MTR station in the Northern District. As it was not possible to have large scale demonstrations, Streambreaker sat down on the ground to stage his own silent protest. He held his hands up in the '5+1' (Five Demands, Not One Less) protest gesture. "I felt then that this was the only thing I could do. I didn't expect I would attract the attention of some passers-by who came up to me with food and drinks. One even gave me bubble milk tea! This solo protest of mine also attracted two strangers to join me. A woman and a student who was carrying a basketball or possibly a football sat with me from twelvish to five-ish in the afternoon. When they left, they asked me to leave with them. And I did.'

On October 6, there was an 'Anti-emergency act demonstration' followed by another similar one on October 12. Streambreaker attended them all. He even got a lift home in a 'parent's car' and another 'parent' gave him an unregistered SIM card. He said it would be safer using it. On October 13, there were these citywide protests in all 18 districts. Streambreaker was using a mobile with the given SIM card, and he went to different areas to 'refurbish'[2] pro-China shops and companies. Once when he was leaving a mall after this activity, he ran into a group of anti-riot police. As there were railings blocking his way to the road in front, he instinctively veered into the right side of the road instead of jumping over the railings. "I didn't know there was a police car on the right and so I was trapped."

Streambreaker and the other protesters who were running with him could only try escaping through the exit of a carpark. But when he ran up to it, he realised it was a dead end. Some protesters tried climbing over the wire fence, but they were beaten down by the police who used batons to beat their legs. "I

---

2   The expression *"to refurbish"* was a euphemism used during the Anti-ELAB Movement to refer to vandalising public facilities or commercial enterprises which the protesters took to be run by "red" (CCP-related) or "deep blue" (those having a clear pro-government stance) businesspersons or corporations.

tried to escape out of the car park via a different route. Initially I managed to break through two police defence lines, but when I arrived at the third, I was caught."

Before he was bundled into the police car, the only thing that Streambreaker could do was shout out his name loudly to the crowd gathered. He realised afterwards that a legislative councillor who was present at that time heard him call out his name and passed it on. His schoolmates got news of his arrest and detainment on October 13 from some unknown sources. They tried to organise a sit-in support action on October 14. "I didn't know exactly what they did as I was sent to a hospital for the injuries I sustained on my limbs after I was beaten by the police. Luckily there was no fracture."

Streambreaker was released on October 15. The principal of his school told him that after his arrest, many schoolmates messaged his form-teacher and asked about his condition. "The first time when I was arrested, I told one teacher about it. She was trying very hard to hold back her tears then. Therefore, I decided not to tell any other teachers as I didn't want them to get upset." But this second time, news of his arrest spread throughout the whole school.

Throughout the movement, Streambreaker acted mostly on his own. He was therefore rather indifferent towards this mass support from his schoolmates. His response showed a maturity beyond his age. "To me, it's very easy to write a card of comfort or encouragement. Just verbally saying they are behind me and yet are not willing to physically take part in the movement. That is useless!" He pauses and then continues, "I spotted some classmates in the August 31 protest. So, I know roughly who had been out on the streets." He has also run into a schoolmate from another class on October 13. "But they all left early. It was only me who stayed till very late and ended up being arrested." Streambreaker felt that most of his schoolmates only rendered him verbal support, but no real action sprang from there. Someone did start a human chain activity and a class boycott. But they were all pre-approved by the school.

Both of Streambreaker's arrests resulted in him being charged. It was hard for him to say how to proceed from this point. When he was bailed after his first arrest, the lawyer suggested to him that he had to be much more careful in future. But on his second arrest, the lawyer told him not to take to the streets again. Streambreaker understands the risk involved but reckons that he can still "try doing a bit". He believes that *"there's indeed a kind of responsibility when one is born into a chaotic time"*.[3] This saying is not a mere empty promise.

---

3 This slogan ("生於亂世，有種責任", in Chinese) was popular in the 2014 Umbrella Movement.

"There needs to be some accompanying proactive actions if we want to extend our influence."

He is worried that once he becomes lax, he will forget his "original intention". "If I don't keep up with the development of the movement, even to the extent of forgetting it, will I revert to my political apathetic self?" He does not want to see that happening. "I then decided to carry on helping to maintain the Lennon Walls and to take part only in more peaceful activities." He started with the Lennon Wall near home "with the hope that his effort would extend to similar walls in other districts."

Streambreaker has been arrested on two occasions and is facing three criminal charges. He expects that he will not be charged on at least one of them. It is not known how things will develop. The happenings in these past few months in 2019 and his eventual arrests have caused an even greater alienation in Streambreaker's already strained relationship with his family. "Long before these events, our relationship has never been harmonious. Before the movement, I would stay overnight in video games centres instead of going home. But I have not taken up smoking or drinking." He admits spending nights in video games centres has been an 'over the top' behaviour. Maybe it is this trait in him that explains why as a secondary student, he has such guts to be a front-line protester.

> My parents were very autocratic in the past, so I reacted strongly to their strict discipline and my stringent upbringing. After my arrests, they adopted a couldn't-care-less attitude. Now when we are all at home, we don't even talk to each other. We don't communicate with each other face to face. Even when we have meals, we don't sit down and eat at the same time nor at the same table. Our relationship has worsened. We are more estranged from each other.

Streambreaker confesses that he used to be politically apathetic. It is the Liberal Studies subject at school that first acquainted him with the extradition law. "I used to think that politics is mere hullabaloo, something that tires one out with its nonsense. But the Liberal Studies teacher tried to discuss with us the extradition bill from the point of view of various stakeholders. Her views were objective. I think she spoke well. I then found myself starting to build and form my own stance and opinions."

Streambreaker analyses how he develops his own set of values. He feels that it was due to the influence of some past incidents. For example, the 'parallel traders' incident, and the Umbrella Movement. But mostly his values have been shaped through his interest in reading books on philosophy when he was in junior secondary school. For example, he has read a book called *'Justice: What's the Right Thing to Do'*. He has also tried attending the on-line philosophy classes of the Harvard Professor Michael Sandel, who wrote this book, but he did not really like these classes much. "I am more acquainted with Martin Luther King's ideas and have been deeply inspired by Malcom X, the African American civil rights leader. I quite subscribe to his ideas. Here's part of what Malcom X said in 1965: We declare our right on this earth to be a man, to be a human being, to be presented as a human being, to be given the rights of a human being in this society, on this earth, in this day, which we intend to bring into existence by any means necessary."

Streambreaker puts great emphasis on the last phrase, "I agree with what Malcom X says about 'by any means necessary', that all necessary actions have to be resorted to." Applying this to the political situation in Hong Kong, he says, "you may say why not communicate with the government first? But when the government just refuses to listen and communicate with its citizens, and if violence is the only way out, one must use it."

Streambreaker further explains, "There was once a philosophy programme on the Hong Kong Radio Station. It talked about the use of love and peaceful methods in a fair society, and these could arouse one's conscience and could influence votes. I agree. But since there's no dual universal suffrage in the Hong Kong electoral system, how can the use of love and peaceful means influence votes?" He puts it simply, "when the government does not want to listen to its citizens, the citizens have to try every means necessary to protest."

He has considered what Malcom X says about 'any means necessary'. "So how can we differentiate between what are necessary means and what are not? I have cast doubts on this and so have been ambivalent about acts like '*si liu*' (extrajudicial punishment) and brick-throwing. I have hesitated about or rejected committing them. If peaceful means can make the society better and are the only necessary means, peace is certainly a good way. But look at Hong Kong, peaceful means have proven to be ineffective. That's why I have chosen to resort to more aggressive ways."

Looking back at these past few months of acute political deterioration induced by the amendment of the anti-extradition law in Hong Kong, Streambreaker chronicles in this manner, "I still believe that dual universal suffrage is most important. If there is genuine election, the legislative councillors can request a thorough investigation into police brutality, and a thorough shake-up of the police force. Influence on politics can then be made. Even though I am not optimistic that this would happen, I have been reminding myself that I act not because of hope, but because hope can only exist when there is action. I am young. I don't have many burdens. I must do whatever I can."

This interview took place in September 2019 and Streambreaker should be sitting the Diploma of Secondary Education (DSE) examinations in half a year's time. Has he given any thoughts to his future studies? "I want to be enrolled in the Philosophy Department of either the Chinese University (CU), Hong Kong University (HKU) or Lingnan University. But I am worried about the credit points. CU requires 23, Lingnan 19 and I have more confidence in getting these results in my DSE exams." Streambreaker is 17 years old, and aside from contemplating the life of an undergraduate, he is at the same time interested in acting and has thought of becoming an actor. But the reality remains that he has been charged. He will appear in court and be on trial later. How will his young life be changed? Streambreaker says, "If you ask me what's been sacrificed ... yes, my future. If I have a criminal record, what impact will it have on my future studies and my career?"

But very soon, Streambreaker remembers some good moments he had experienced during the Movement, "At least I have lived. In the past, Hong Kong people only focused on money. They were very indifferent, but this time I can see their solidarity. I am very touched." He jokes about the belief of some people that protesters have been paid to demonstrate. "Indeed, I have been given HK$500 once, and then bail money from the 612 Humanitarian Relief Fund. An 'elder sister' has given me an old iPhone 6. Also when I was tear-gassed in Yuen Long, I received a free octopus card. When my two mobile phones were in police custody, Spark Alliance let me claim HK$5000 from its fund for a replacement."

When he is telling this dark joke, it is really because he cannot forget the assistance that other people have rendered him. "I didn't attend the protests because I have been paid. It's because of the protests that I ran into all these Hong Kong people, all of whom were ready to help." Streambreaker then adds, in a serious tone, "If anyone lures me with money or other things to take part in any of the protests, I will expose him. This is justice!" He is a mature 17-year-old, but also an innocent one.

CHAPTER 10

Loafer and His Brother Were Arrested: "From That Day On, We Became a Family of 'Martyrs'"

In this family of four, the two brothers were arrested. The maximum sentence could be 10 years for the elder one, whilst it could be life imprisonment for the younger.

The elder brother, Loafer, was arrested first. In streets misted by tear gas, the police's Special Tactical Contingent – a riot team commonly known as the 'Raptors' – charged at him, 4 to 1. What follows is the usual story: he was taken into custody; he waited; got to an arraignment hearing only after more than 50 hours; was released on bail; got home; then had an even longer wait for the trial. During the long wait for the trial, Loafer's little brother was also arrested in another context. The whole family went through the same process again.

How did this ordinary Hong Kong family get entangled in this fateful summer of 2019? If we go back in time to look at their father's story, we might be able to add another footnote to this revolution of our times.

• • •

"My father doesn't like the CCP [Chinese Communist Party]. He really doesn't like it," said Loafer.

Loafer's grandfather was a member of the Kuomintang Party. After the rise of the CCP, he was persecuted and escaped to Hong Kong. "My grandpa hated the CCP. He hated it so much that every time the national anthem was played on a television channel, he would switch it off. Once he saw news relating to the CCP, he would start swearing," recounted Loafer. He felt that this subtly influenced his father, whilst he himself was more 'rational'. "I love my country but not the Party. I like China as a place with beautiful scenery. I can separate China from the CCP and look at it in different ways."

Loafer was born in mainland China. His mother is also mainland Chinese. He used to go to a school which taught in Mandarin Chinese. "The application to come to Hong Kong was only approved when I was in kindergarten. But mum's visa wasn't approved until later." It was only in 2003 that his family finally reunited in Hong Kong. Why does Loafer remember so vividly that it was 2003? "Because my whole family, including my maternal grandmother, who's always been in mainland China, joined the July 1st march [that year]. My dad got her to go as well. He wanted her to see what it was like."

Loafer was only five back then and had no recollection of the march. He continued, "I only found out as mum and dad talked about it and we've kept photos from that day." It was really quite something for a father to bring his young son, wife, and mother-in-law from the mainland to participate in a 500,000-people-strong march against Article 23 in 2003. Sixteen years later this same father became embroiled in the Anti-ELAB Movement. The magnitude, form, situation, and costs were totally different this time. This must have given the father real heartache. "Dad also joined the march against the Extradition Law. He's quite supportive of the Movement. Later on, he learnt that I was kind of at the forefront of it, and he told me to be more careful," Loafer said.

As for his mother, her situation is rather like the many 'old' new immigrants to Hong Kong. "Mum has close relations in mainland China and so naturally she cares about it. But things like adulterated food scandals in China disgust her." Because of his mum's mainland ties, Loafer travels to mainland China from time to time. In contrast to some young people who have no emotional connection to China at all, mainland China does not feel foreign to him. "I still went to China from time to time before 2019, not now of course. Even if I wanted to go, I wouldn't be able to get through the border [now]."

The education system in Hong Kong has not 'brainwashed' Loafer at all. He has felt a connection with mainland China with his relatives living there. The Hong Kong government pushed for a revamp of the 'Liberal Studies' subject, attributing Hong Kong students' lack of patriotism to its curriculum. But what we see in Loafer is a different story. "We have to study Chinese History in the first three years of secondary school. That gives us a broad understanding of China. Liberal studies, and information on the internet all make me feel that China is a good place. It has a very rich and attractive culture. You can see that's why so many foreigners come to China to understand more about its history. It really has its appeal."

Without noticing it himself, Loafer repeatedly said that he loved the country, but not the governing party, the CCP. How did this sentiment come about? Loafer recalled what he saw in mainland China when he was young. "You frequently see propaganda slogans in Mainland China, the likes of 'Travel in a civilised manner', 'Be a civilised person', 'Build a civilised China'. This feels like China being strong on the outside but weak inside, that everything is too superficial. If the general population had received proper education, you just wouldn't have had to stress this kind of thing."

He felt increasing unease after watching clips on the internet about the Great Leap Forward – an economic and social campaign led by the CCP from 1958 to 1962 during which Mao 'encouraged' peasants to live together in collective farms, then the June-Fourth Massacre, and other Chinese historical events. "You can see repression of various sorts ... During the Second Sino-Japanese War, the Kuomintang [literally, the Chinese Nationalist Party] were the ones who fought the war, whereas the CCP just claimed the credit. In the end, the Nationalists were forced to retreat to Taiwan. The more I read about what had happened, the more it disgusts me."

Loafer started gradually to learn more about China through the news, instead of being restricted to "*Huaxia* civilization" (i.e., civilization of the Chinese nation) education in school. "In mainland China, too many people vanish just because of what they have said. The state can simply make up anything haphazardly – like visiting prostitutes – just to incriminate and arrest anyone. This can only fuel distrust of the Party and its legal system."

He mentioned the disappearance of the five booksellers from Causeway Bay Books in 2015.[1] Loafer was still in secondary school back then, but the incident was imprinted in his memory. "The bookstore was said to be selling banned books. Then the booksellers were abducted by some clandestine speedboats and were forced to confess in video footage [on the mainland]. I feel it was just a 'show'." He thinks that it was done to instil fear in people in the mainland because the Party wanted too much to '*save face*'. He even made this analogy, "This is no different from terrorists killing people and forcing them to kneel to make a film to be made public."

Regarding pre-2019 Hong Kong, Loafer has pent-up discontent with livelihood issues. "The government invested in many white elephant projects. Like the scandal about the Shatin-Central link railway extension, in which construction work and materials were substandard, and metal bars were found to be cut shorter than required; yet the government didn't see any problem. The construction of one bridge [Hong Kong-Zhuhai-Macau Bridge] cost more

---

1   Five staff members of the Causeway Bay Books, an independent bookshop in Hong Kong specialising in books on China, disappeared in suspicious circumstances between October and December 2015. At least two vanished in mainland China, and one in Thailand. Another one disappeared from Hong Kong without the necessary travel documents. Lam Wing-kee, the founder of the bookstore, eventually came back to Hong Kong after eight months of detention in China. He gave a press conference in which he spoke about his abduction, his scripted confession, and similar video-recorded confessions of his associates. This abduction of Hong Kong residents by the Central Investigation Team under direct control of Beijing authorities sent shock waves across Hong Kong and internationally. Eventually Lam left Hong Kong and emigrated to Taiwan, feeling that it was no longer safe for him to stay in the territory.

than a hundred billion;[2] you could have built a US naval fleet with that much money."

Loafer thinks that building a bridge with few users was just a way to transfer money to mainland China. "It brings suspicion that the project is an avenue to transfer benefits. On top of that, installation of 'smart lampposts' just intensifies public resentment of the Hong Kong government in its coupling with China."

Loafer opines that the escalating hatred of the government sprung from the steady erosion of Hong Kong's way of life. "Hong Kong was like the frog in the slow boil in the past. I can't say I didn't have my discontent. I just turned a blind eye to it. There were people voicing out back then, but it was never as radical as it is now. It was never like so many people now coming out [to express their discontent]." He said that after the anti-national education protest (in 2012) and government's subsequent withdrawal of the curriculum,[3] things died down. Hong Kong people toed the line and basically returned to their old way of life.

By the time of the Umbrella Movement in 2014, Loafer was in junior secondary school. He did not take part in it or know much about it. "I went to Admiralty and Mongkok with school friends once. It was a shocking sight to see busy roads turned into a sea of tents. Everyone worked together and gave their best towards a common goal. I was only there to observe; I didn't join them."

Since 1997, Hong Kong has been through several large-scale social movements and protests. All ended eventually with 'life returning to normal', or perhaps just as Loafer said about 'the frog in the slow boil'. Everyone at first looked at the Anti-ELAB Movement with similar thoughts. However, there was a subtle difference this time, which led to a drastically different result as it went completely out of control. Loafer voiced his opinion, "Carrie Lam's administration was different from previous ones. She insisted on riding roughshod over

---

2　According to media reports as per LegCo documents, the government had spent HKD 120.1 bn up to 2018 on the construction of the Hong Kong-Zhuhai-Macau Bridge. See Lam Cho Wai, "Politics override professionalism? Five controversies ignited by the 100 billion plus Hong Kong-Zhuhai-Macau Bridge in Hong Kong", BBC (Chinese), 19 Oct 2018, https://www.bbc.com /zhongwen/trad/chinese-news-45898013 (in Chinese, last viewed 15 Sept 2022). Up till then, the HK government has already applied to LegCo for more than 120 billion for works related to the construction of the bridge.

3　The Education Bureau issued the Moral and National Education curriculum in early 2012. Several pressure groups were formed to oppose it, the most prominent one being Scholarism, founded by a group of secondary students in 2011. In July 2012, an alliance of 15 such organisations was formed to launch protests against the curriculum. Scholarism began an occupation of the grounds of the Government Headquarters on 30 August, and this, together with mass gatherings as well as a series of hunger strikes, only ended in the early hours of 9 September, hours after the Chief Executive, Leung Chun-ying, announced withdrawal of the curriculum.

everyone. Instead of boiling a frog in tepid water, she turned the heat high up. The Anti-ELAB Movement began only with people's disagreement and discontent with the government. But after June and July [2019], with the government's complete disregard of Hong Kong people's livelihoods and welfare to curry favour with mainland China, even to the extent of supporting the police force blindly, the initial discontent gradually turned into hatred of the government."

• • •

And then it was February 2019. On grounds of Taiwan's request for the extradition of Chan Tong-Kai, a Hong Kong citizen, for the murder of Poon Hiu-Wing in Taipei, Hong Kong Government's Security Bureau proposed a controversial bill which would allow extraditions from Hong Kong to both Taiwan and mainland China. Since then, Hong Kong has become a different place, and Loafer and his family's fortune is closely linked to that of Hong Kong. "At the beginning I was simply paying more attention to its development and didn't participate in any protests. On 9 June, I went out to protest together with a group of friends," Loafer said. On that day, a million Hong Kong people took to the streets; that night, the government published a press release at 11 pm, saying that people's different views on various issues were acknowledged and respected, but the second reading debate on the Bill would resume on 12 June regardless. Loafer continued, "The Government's response stoked up the sentiments of some protesters. There were protesters gathering at the Legislative Council's designated demonstration area – I was there too, but we were just shouting slogans and did no violent acts at all."

Loafer said he was not really at the forefront at that time; rather he was watching from a distance. Suddenly five to six 'Raptors' came out from nowhere, while uniformed officers had the protesters at the centre surrounded. Loafer had turned into a 'sentinel' unintentionally, communicating situation updates from the outside. He had somehow become the police's target as he was separated from his friends. "They were chasing after us, from the designated demonstration area all the way to the Ferris Wheel [on the waterfront]." From then on, Loafer had 'come out', taking part in many protests and becoming increasingly part of the forefront.

June 12 marked the first time Loafer was ever exposed to tear gas. "I could say that I was at the forefront by then. At that time, we didn't have much sense about how to fight. We simply set up barricades when we saw the police and told people behind us to leave." The situation was still like this by mid-July. Back then, being at the forefront was to ensure other protesters evacuated in time, and persistent protesters were pulled away. Everyone at the scene would consciously take up different tasks – barricade setup, organising supplies, first aid, etc. In other words, 'being at the forefront' at that time had the goal of arranging escape routes for everybody. "The police back then weren't over the top yet. You still had time to pull away those who insisted on staying. But there was not a chance later; the first thing the police came out and did was to pin you down," said Loafer.

At the time of the 7.21 Incident, Loafer was in Western District on Hong Kong Island, at the frontline. He could not get to Yuen Long in time to help. On 27 July, he was there when protesters gathered to 'reclaim' Yuen Long. Many protesters were arrested by riot police in the conflict that night; some were injured, fainted, and left big pools of blood on the road. "It was shocking to see this first-hand at the scene, and there wasn't much I could do." At that point he felt very sad for others; little did he know that he would be arrested at a protest scene the next day.

Loafer said he was "unlucky". He was in Western District on that day where protesters had split up into two groups. He was in a quiet street, planning to retreat. Suddenly the riot police fired tear gas and pushed forward. The protesters had been ambushed from all directions and the police were arresting them. Loafer, standing at the frontline, was pushed, and pinned down by four or five Raptors. "They knocked you with their shield. If you didn't fall there and then, you would be clubbed by police batons. Thankfully I still had my helmet on – the helmet I used in war games – it gave very good protection. My head, and shoulders were clubbed, the back of my head too – it was swollen."

On this night, in this place, some were arrested, and some had a narrow escape.

For the 44 who could not escape in time, their fate was linked up with that of Hong Kong, both equally dark and uncertain. Loafer and the other 43 were sent to be detained in a police station in the New Territories. "If they were to detain us close by, other protesters could have surrounded the police station." He was arrested after dark, sent to the hospital due to his injuries from being clubbed, and was taken back to the police station not until three in the morning. Tens of people in their group were rounded up in an indoor car park to wait. "The covered car park, with the metal gate rolled down, was just cramped." After 12 hours' wait, it was 3 pm the next day when he was sent to a stinky detention room. "If you wanted to use the loo, you had to ask the officers an hour before. They just kept saying, 'Yeah, just wait.'"

It was already the third morning after his arrest before Loafer could see his solicitor. At 8-ish that evening, the police suddenly said they had to search his house. He insisted that his solicitor had to be there, but his call to the solicitor did not go through. The police told him, "It doesn't matter. We just go ahead and will finish the search very quickly." Despite Loafer's insistence, it was not smooth sailing, and eventually the search was done in his solicitor's presence. Loafer recalled, "It was midnight. My family were home too. The police sent in their Narcotics Bureau to do the search."

After being detained for over 30 hours, everyone looked at their watch, felt a bit relaxed and discussed whether they should 'refuse to be bailed', or 'be released on bail'. At that point they just thought, "They could not be charged. The police were just messing with them for at most 48 hours, after which the worst-case scenario would be being charged with Unlawful Assembly." That was Hong Kong in July; most Hongkongers still held on to this naïve thinking without realising that calamity was imminent.

Feeling composed in this thought, the first one in the room was called over, and he came back with two charges. "He's the first one being called over. He returned with two sheets of paper, one charged for rioting, and the other for assaulting police officers." After that, two were called over from each room. For those who had not been called, they still harboured the wishful thinking, "Perhaps two were picked out from each room as a warning to the others." But very soon this logic did not work because the rest of the group were very swiftly called and handed a charge on return. "Everyone was charged with rioting," said Loafer.

Handed the charges, this group of 44, including Loafer, were brought before the judge the next day. Their naïve wish of just being 'messed with' had turned into despair. The city's atmosphere and approach to many things had drastically changed overnight: Hong Kong had entered a new era, an era in which urgency to arrest and charge took precedence over the presumption of innocence.

From that day on, Loafer is not his old self anymore; he is the Loafer with a riot charge. "Did I go out again after that? Yes, I did, though I stayed at the back. Perhaps it was because the charge really got to me ... or perhaps I was feeling tired and just needed a break." He did join subsequent 'human chains', 'wo lei fei'[4] events, etc. "I still wanted to support and show strength in numbers, so I went."

During this time, Loafer's family got caught up in turmoil by the destiny of Hong Kong again. Loafer only had class in the afternoon that day. His brother left home for school early in the morning. Within 30 seconds, the doorbell rang. He thought his brother might have forgotten his keys. Once he opened

---

4   *Wo lei fei*, in Cantonese, literally "peaceful, rational, and non-violent", refers to those protest-ers who insisted on using peaceful, non-violent means. This is referred to as PRN in Part One.

the door, he saw his brother held in custody by a few policemen behind. "The policemen hid themselves in the back stairs earlier. They had the warrant and started searching the house right away."

Being a bystander watching the search unfold that day, Loafer felt it somehow scarier than the time when he himself was involved. "It was completely out of the blue. The police seized a bag, a pair of trousers, etc. as evidence." His brother was also brought before a judge the next day. "From this day on, we have become a family of 'martyrs'," Loafer made this comment at the scene, but no one could laugh at all.

Loafer's brother, who is still in secondary school, was charged with a very serious crime. "The maximum sentence can be life imprisonment. They said his assault was intentional and premeditated. Mum and Dad were worried sick." Loafer did not say a lot about how his parents felt, but he did frankly say he worried more about his little brother than himself. "I was just standing there and didn't do anything. The police said they had video clips of me. What they saw was just me standing. But my little brother ... CCTV in the MTR, shopping malls. All captured his face and what he did."

Loafer guessed that someone snitched on his brother, or the police found him through facial identification technology even though he had his face mask on. "That was bizarre. CCTV only captured half his face, then the police hid next to our residence and managed to get him. When they were searching our home, they took away a pair of trousers, trainers, and his backpack. There were a couple of watches on my desk; they were mine, not my brother's, but still they picked one to take away. They just didn't want to miss anything and took more than they had to."

So, dragged on by the wheel of time, the two brothers are entangled in the turmoil. "We are both on bail. He doesn't go out as much, but still does at times, stealthily. Mom and Dad don't know about it. He doesn't want them to worry."

After that, there were many worsening and baffling news headlines. Loafer could not help but compare those to his own situation. "Look at the knife attack at the 'Lennon Wall' message board in Tseung Kwan O. The charge brought by the prosecution was only common assault. Why would my brother be charged with intentional assault? That guy used a knife; my brother used his bare fist. How about the white-shirted triads in Yuen Long on 7.21? There were loads of photographic evidence. Why would I be the one being charged with rioting instead of them?" But what worries Loafer most is still his little brother.

• • •

Sometimes Loafer would look back to the day when he was in custody. "At the beginning we didn't feel fearful with the 44 of us sitting together. On the contrary, we were pretty calm and had a good chat together." By the time most of them had been charged and released on bail, and there were less of them in the detention room, fear began to creep in. "I started feeling scared ... and imagining bad things."

Finally, there were only two of them remaining in the room: Loafer and a social worker. "I think I am quite an optimistic person. But at that time, I was filled with negative thoughts. For a split second I thought death could have put an end to everything." The social worker sitting by his side at the time told him simply and firmly, "You have done nothing wrong." It is her words that have stayed with him through these many days. "Her words have been my support all through these times, my support until now."

Despite 'blue ribbons' beside him and the police calling them names like 'cockroaches', 'rioters' and even accusing "them of being troublemakers worthy of dying", Loafer, at the same time, remembers his fellow brothers and sisters in arms in campaigns, and remembers these words: "We are not wrong, we have done nothing wrong; we do this for ourselves [our future]."

This is how he looks at the ordeal of his arrest and the price he paid. "To play a part in a revolution, I need to be mentally prepared for the possibility of arrest when I come out. This is a sacrifice that must be made. It's just that it happened to me, and it's my fate." Loafer is very young in our eyes, but in his eyes, there are many younger people making their sacrifices too. "I saw teenagers being arrested and felt such heartache. I was thinking why we couldn't protect them."

He tries to make sense of his own sacrifice; only through this can he face his life ahead. He also tries to make sense of Hong Kong people's situation in the Movement of the past six months. "We are connected. I haven't seen Hong Kong as united as this before. One million, two million, ethnic minorities, new immigrants, everyone came together to express what they wanted. Hongkongers are now connected. This makes me feel really content and it's such a comforting thought: we are united."

With unprecedented connectedness there is also a hint of unprecedented loss. What came to Loafer's mind right away is not his own future, however. "Loss ... I just can't put it in words. I feel that something is missing deep down in my heart. Maybe it's Hong Kong, our home. We are losing it bit by bit." Loafer paused, then continued, "I really love this place."

CHAPTER 11

Henry: "As a Hongkonger, I Did What I Had to Do"

Over 40 years of age, Henry graduated from university in 1997, an ordinary person coming across this "great time". He did not choose the "great time", but the "great time" chose him. Henry feels that the beliefs and the values that he upholds today were influenced by the Christian "fellowship activities" he participated in while he was at school. The discussions about religion and philosophies at that time in the fellowship by the group of hot-blooded youngsters did not dissipate over time, but instead remained deeply imprinted on his life.

In Hong Kong, going to Christian fellowship is very common among youngsters. However, in a society with the largest population being Chinese, Christian fellowship being popular was probably a unique phenomenon in Hong Kong, given its special historical background. Now, some 20 years later, after witnessing the ups and downs of 2019, Henry thought carefully back to those days gone by and realised that there might have been a connection between the two. "In those days of fellowship, we discussed a great deal about issues between religion and politics, and the most important thing about the fellowship was that it nurtured a concern for society." He said that the gospel could not be separated from society, nor could it be spread purely by passing on the message verbally. When there is unfairness and injustice in a society and its system, "we have to do what we have to do."

"I did what I had to do" Henry generously shared with us his story. As he recounted the story, he remembered the sensation of spasms in the lungs when he coughed. The traumas at Citic Tower and that night in Yuen Long have followed him like shadows, never leaving. At around 2.30 pm on June 12, Henry was at Admiralty with a friend who was an ambulance man with the disciplined services. They heard that the riot police had arrived. They saw that the young people were all putting on their helmets and their goggles, and they both knew that it was time to retreat. Just before they left, Henry handed the long umbrella he was carrying to the demonstrators there and just at that time, someone shouted, 'Ambulance Man!'

> My pal was an ambulance man, a real ambulance man, and when he heard the cry, how could he just leave? Just like that, it was as if fate had led us, we went to the medical station (the roundabout outside the entrance to the Legislative Council Building). My friend immediately gave first aid to people, and I helped as some sort of general helper.

At that very moment, the riot police started using pepper spray, and soon after, they fired the first tear gas canister. And when the police started shooting, Henry and his friend became officially 'involved' ... "My friend and I wore only ordinary face masks, we weren't prepared at all," Henry said.

When everyone retreated and moved the supplies to a 'legal' spot – the defined legal area in the Civil Human Rights Front's application to the police for the protest, which was the entrance to Citic Tower, Henry saw that the tear gas shots were being aimed at the medical station, and two of the booths were wrecked, including where he and his friend were, and where they had been before. "There was no way we could stay, we really had to leave, and we intended to go inside Citic Tower to try and find a way out." There, they saw a young man inside, and his leg seemed to have been broken. He was lying on the floor and he was having difficulty breathing, while his body was convulsing. "When we saw that, how could we leave? We simply did not have the heart to leave him."

They went to help. At that time, more and more people rushed inside the building. "The scene was frightening, very frightening ... I had really wanted to take out my mobile phone to take photos, as I felt I needed to record the evidence, but subconsciously I felt I couldn't show other people's faces. I was terrified there; it was just like war."

They heard, coming from the outside, 'Bang! Bang! Bang!': the police were firing tear gas incessantly. In front of them it was all thick smoke, and people kept rushing in from the outside. "If we went to the third floor, we could go through Café de Coral (a fast-food chain store), and then out onto the footbridge. That ought to be the only way out, as all the other exits were blocked. But faced with the young man who had broken his leg, we had to stay, how could we leave?"

Clouds of choking smoke kept coming in. The whole Citic Tower was shrouded in brown smoke, and the vision became blurry. "I was wearing my goggles and I could see almost nothing. I only knew that the riot police were nearby and that was frightening." Henry and his friend decided to transport the young man with broken bones away from the spot. His friend, the ambulance man, found a sheet of very hard cardboard to try and fix his leg, and then lifted him up and moved him. Another volunteer came to help. "There were four of us, each taking a corner and we carried him one level up to inspect the situation there. There was still a lot of heavy smoke, and everyone was coughing non-stop. The coughing was so bad it was like having asthma, and we felt that if we continued to cough like that, we would simply collapse."

Henry was watching the young man with the broken leg, and he was not sure if he had fainted. He was very scared, and his heart was pounding very fast, as if it was going to pop out. "I was terrified, terrified that someone would die." Henry was afraid that the riot police would rush in any time. They had no time to ponder, and they simply carried the young man up two levels. While they were carrying the young man, some people started to scream. It was extremely chaotic, and because of the thick smoke, Henry somehow got separated from his friend and the young man. 'It sounds impossible, but I did get separated from them. The vision was very blurry, I didn't know where they'd gone."

It was the first time Henry experienced tear gas indoors, and the situation was terrifying. Also, no one was mentally prepared for it. "There were many young girls, and some started to have asthma attacks, and slumped against the columns. Then someone who had gone outside returned to lead the others out."

After the Citic Tower incident on June 12, Henry became a witness to history again in the evening of July 21 in Yuen Long. He was not an indigenous inhabitant of the New Territories, but he had lived in Yuen Long for 20 years. That day, rumours circulated about a planned attack by people wearing white, and Henry became very anxious. After dinner, he went to Kai Tei[1] and experienced the second trauma in the Anti-ELAB Movement.

> On July 21, it was circulated on Facebook that, at dusk, large numbers of people wearing white would gather. So, after dinner, I took pains to change into casual clothing worn by people who live in the neighbourhood and went to Kai Tei at approximately 9 pm. I wanted to see if the men-in-white had left and intended to report it on Facebook if I saw anything.

Arriving at Kai Tei, Henry found there were indeed a lot of men-in-white gathered around. He roamed about near them, trying to eavesdrop on their conversations, but all along he did not dare switch on his mobile phone. On the one hand he was afraid that the light from the mobile phone would alert them, on the other hand he saw people taking photos with their mobile phones, and they were immediately shouted at and beaten by those elderly men-in-white. "It was scary," he said.

> I was in my casual neighbourhood attire, and I was walking around among them. I heard that they weren't speaking Putonghua, but the

---

1   Kai Tei, literally, "chicken land", is a south-east spot in what is now central Yuen Long, and it used to be where poultry trading was done. Now, it is just adjacent to the Yuen Long metro station, where the notorious "7.21 Incident" occurred, when triad members clad in white T-shirts beat up passengers and pedestrians in the station.

local dialect. I deliberately eavesdropped, and at that time, a private car drove past on the road. There were several people inside and the men-in-white commented, 'Isn't that So and So Sir?'[2] Their general conversations referred to a police officer sitting inside the car, and it was obvious that some of the men-in-white knew that 'Sir'.

At nearly 10 pm, Henry went to a bakery shop in Kai Tei and pretended to buy something. He stayed a little while, as he wanted to eavesdrop and to observe those men-in-white, to see whether they had any plans to attack people. During that period, no black-clad youths[3] walked past, just a man and a woman in black clothes on their way somewhere. But it was calm, and he did not feel anything would happen.

Heading toward Yuen Long Station, Henry saw on the way some people who could have been social workers or volunteers standing at different locations. "From the looks of mutual concern in our eyes, I knew that everyone was there to help. That image was deeply ingrained in my memory; the look of knowing each other, I will never forget."

However, when he arrived at Yuen Long Station, that was a completely different scene. In the lobby and the platforms were piles of clothes for people to change into. Three people on the platforms were calling out, urging those in black who had come back from the demonstrations elsewhere to quickly change out of their black clothing, for fear that they had not seen the Telegram messages warning of the imminent attack, and would thus be in danger. Some heeded the call and changed clothes immediately; some felt there was no need to feel anxious, but on the whole, these were the minority.

Sometime between 10.00 pm and 10.30 pm, Henry was intending to go through the station turnstile to depart, seeing that nothing extraordinary seemed to be happening. Right at that moment, he heard people calling out loudly. He turned back to look. There were a young man and a young woman, both in black. There were two men-in-white chasing them and starting to beat them. The men-in-white rushed in through the entrance connecting Yoho Mall and Yuen Long Station. Henry immediately took out his mobile phone and started filming and taking photographs, and at the same time he was chasing after them and telling them not to beat people. Henry recalled,

---

2 An informal polite address, normally used in Hong Kong and South China for policemen.
3 The protesters normally dressed in black mainly to make it harder for individual identification.

The situation at that time was that two men-in-white were chasing and hitting the young man, and the young woman was by the side and was calling out, 'Why do you beat people?'

The men-in-white continued to chase through the turnstile, so he followed suit. The young woman and Henry tried to stop the men-in-white who were holding wooden sticks.

I recalled when I was in Kai Tei earlier, I also saw men-in-white holding wooden and rattan sticks. That wooden stick was about one inch in diameter.

After going through the turnstile, several men-in-white pushed the young man towards the wall. When they were about two metres from the wall, they hit the young man with the wooden stick. Henry commented, "The young man looked rather fragile, absolutely not the ferocious type. The wooden stick broke upon hitting him on the body, the broken half flying towards me, and it hit me." The part of Henry's leg where the stick hit immediately bled, and was bruised. "I was only hit by a flying broken wooden stick, yet I ached the whole night and limped when I walked. You can imagine how the young man bled after he had been hit on the head."

The two men-in-white sped off immediately after they had hit the young man. Henry and other people went to the MTR Customer Service Counter and asked the staff there if they had any first aid supplies. During that time some people had called the police, but the police did not come, whereas the ambulance men arrived very quickly. Then a train arrived at the platform; there were many men-in-black and other demonstrators. Henry and other people yelled at them desperately, "Don't go through the turnstiles until you have changed your clothes, there are people beating people down there!" However, the people in black were not too concerned. They did not want to turn back, and they wanted to talk to those men-in-white.

The men-in-black from several trains ended up gathering to give each other courage. At the time, more and more men-in-white were coming into the station. Then Lam Cheuk-ting, a member of North District Council and a Democratic Party LegCo member arrived. Henry did not want to leave. He was standing next to the wall where the beating had taken place; he wanted to protect the evidence. "So, I just stood quietly next to the broken wooden stick. I was naively waiting for the police to arrive, so they could collect the evidence. I didn't dare move; I didn't dare touch the evidence. Huh Huh ...," he laughed self-deprecatingly. Of course, the police never arrived.

In the beginning, people from both sides (men-in-white and men-in-black) were arguing, confronting each other on either side of the turnstiles, very similar to the images that one could see on television news that night. Many people called the police, but there was no response. Many people pressed the alarm bells, and some men-in-black turned on the fire hoses at the men-in-white. Then there were more and more people gathering in both camps, and they were yelling and shouting against the other side. Henry said, "Because I was slightly injured, I took a step back, as I wanted to take a rest. Seeing that the situation was likely to deteriorate, and in order not to get injured and to avoid becoming involved unintentionally, I wanted to leave at this moment."

When Henry walked towards the platform, those men-in-white rushed inside through the turnstiles, and at this time, when they rushed in, the men-in-black could only run towards the platforms. The platforms were on the second level. A train was stopping there, so Henry immediately ran inside the compartment, stood towards the right side of the door, and was submerged among the people. At this critical, historical moment, Henry experienced the 10 minutes of men-in-white beating people standing near the doors of the train carriage, and these were exactly the images that people saw later on television. They were hitting people primarily in two locations. It was more crowded where Lam Cheuk-ting was, with more passengers there.

Henry stood more towards the back, behind two people. He felt very bad, because it turned out that they were shielding him from the relentless attacks. There were many young people on the train. Beside Henry stood an elderly lady and a young girl and they were crouching together. He turned on his mobile phone to film. What he saw was the same that everyone saw on television news: men-in-white continually hitting out at people. What not many people talked about was the sound of airguns shooting. "I filmed for a long time, and even though the resolution was low, you could see lots of small white stuff flying past. They were shot towards the interiors of the compartment from the outside by the men-in-white. I didn't know what they were, but I also heard shooting sounds: 'fut fut fut.'"

Henry could not control his grieved voice, "An elderly man was standing right in front of me at the time. His hair was all white and he was wearing the genuine, casual neighbourhood clothes, neither in white nor in black, yet he was hit by the men-in-white and was beaten so hard that his head bled, and he stayed crouching down." The people in the front said to the men-in-white, "It's not that we didn't want to leave, but the train just wouldn't start!" They spoke with a pleading tone. Henry was still filming, so he knew it was a full ten-minute and the train just did not start. "My mobile phone was on all this time, so I was certain about the duration. From the time I saw the first man-in-white arriving at Yuen Long Station to the train finally closing its doors, it was a total of two and a half hours, from 8.40 pm to 11.15 pm," Henry said with a broken heart. No police came to the scene.

> The ten minutes that the men-in-white were beating people at the doors to the train compartments were very long; it was just like waiting for death.

The doors closed, and the train finally left Yuen Long, and arrived at Long Ping. People in the compartment discussed what to do next. There was the elderly man with a broken head, who was bleeding profusely, and Henry and other witnesses had to send him to seek medical care at Tin Shui Wai. Another elderly lady said she was living in Yuen Long, so Henry got off the train with her, and he called a taxi at Long Ping Station to take her home. "I myself went home, but I did not dare return to Yuen Long, and I immediately forwarded the video to the media," said Henry.

Having experienced the terrifying events on June 12 and July 21 in a few short months and having been beaten and injured by the men-in-white, Henry still insisted on going out to provide support, and was mainly responsible for work such as "safe houses"[4] and "school buses".[5] He had not partnered with his friends to participate in the Movement. "The partners every time were not necessarily the same; the matching was just random. I would meet some people through Telegram, and we usually just worked individually upon arrival at the scene," he said.

Looking back at what happened in those few months, Henry thought that the root of this Movement was people's concern for society. He himself had nurtured this concern for society when he participated in Christian fellowship activities while at school. At the time, a group of young people discussed many topics relating to religion and politics, and they were actively participating in many social movements. He had helped a Legislative Councillor (Frederick Fung) at an election as early as when he was in Form 5 (Year 11). "I graduated from college in 1997, and Hong Kong was facing a lot of political issues at the

---

4 A "safe house" is a temporary shelter for young protesters. Some of them were driven out by their family, and some were afraid that the police would arrest them at home, so they did not dare go home.

5 The "school bus" refers to vehicles of volunteer drivers taking protesters away from the sites of demonstrations. This was necessary because the protests usually ended too late, and all public transport had stopped, or because towards the mid and late stages of the Movement, the MTR would often close some of its stations or would stop operating altogether.

time, such as the Provisional Legislative Council. So whenever we gathered together, we talked about these issues," said Henry.

As a Christian, Henry felt that spreading the gospel and concern for society could not be separated. "The [Christian] gospel includes concern for the community and concern for people. When the social system treats the disadvantaged groups unjustly, we have to do what we have to. As mentioned in the teachings of my faith: even if the world is full of evil and ugly things, even if the results could be tragic, we still must work to preserve or re-build the values of this faith."

The 2014 Umbrella Movement also had the footprints of Henry's positive involvement, as he explained, "I really buy into Benny Tai's concept of love and peace. I was there when the protesters and demonstrators cleared out of Admiralty [the place where protesters gathered] and I had wanted to surrender myself to the police; I was willing to be arrested. Eventually I was persuaded by my friends not to do so. They felt that being arrested would not move the people of Hong Kong and this kind of sacrifice would not have any [meaningful] effect." By the time of the Anti-ELAB Movement in 2019, he had not absented himself.

Henry had thought about his readiness for arrest and incarceration: "I could perhaps withstand imprisonment, but I am averse to pain, and if I were beaten up for no reason, I would be more frightened. It might have been the shadow left behind from July 21 because I saw how ferocious those men-in-white were when they were beating people, and I was in pain for so long with my minor injury."

Although Henry had not given up, he was very pessimistic about whether the Movement would eventually succeed. He said, "I am very pessimistic, and I don't think it will succeed. Universal suffrage for the Chief Executive Council and the Legislative Council was not even worth talking about; I haven't even thought about it. If we could achieve two of the 'Five Demands', withdrawal of the amendment bill and the setting up of an independent commission of inquiry, I would have stopped." He admitted that he saw a lot of hatred in the Movement, and that was the last thing he wanted to see. "I am more inclined to be depressed than feeling hatred; I guess it's got something to do with my religion."

When Henry reflexively informed us of his experiences and feelings, the National Security Act was not yet enacted, the civic organisations were not yet crushed, and the Hong Kong media were still thriving. How this Movement would be viewed and weighed by history, what it means to win or to lose – this needs to be seen and determined by many more people in future.

CHAPTER 12

Elsa: "How a Guardian for Kids Ended Up in Handcuffs"

The Anti-ELAB Movement has not only brought young people into view, but also linked them to the trajectories of numerous elderly individuals. On countless days of street conflict and myriad nights of flaming emotion, Hongkongers of very different ages were active on the sites of demonstrations. Unaware that they were linking up with one another's life courses, they had little idea about the impact they would make on each other. This movement of 2019 unfolded right before Elsa, who was just over 60 years of age. Initially only a bystander with no clue about how to take part, she was handcuffed and arrested by the police in the end. She had come face to face with the danger, the care, and the injuries she experienced at every episode of this process. This is the story of a senior Hongkonger, moving inch by inch into a warzone.

1   Before All This Came About

Born into a big family to illiterate parents, who ran a small business to raise their eight children, Elsa was the only one who liked to read and study. There was an episode about patriotism when she was growing up, but Elsa did not recall much of it, except to say: "Maybe I didn't care for this period, as I did appear to be rather radical back then. While my classmates would carry this part of the memory with them, I could hardly remember anything about it." It turned out that when she was a Form Two (Year 8) secondary school student, a teacher brought the class to the China Week Exhibition organised by the Hong Kong Federation of Students, to enhance their nationalist sentiment. After the visit, as a matter of course, Elsa joined the Federation's Secondary Students Group. She could remember, vaguely, that there were many sub-groups operating under it that ran activities on campus in the mode of a covert underground party. Due to the brevity of her participation as well as perhaps some emotional factors, her memory of this interlude remains very vague.

Living in a cramped traditional *tong-lau*[1] flat, all the children had to help their father to make a living for the family. Despite poverty, her father refused any government subsidy and never applied for public housing. However, Elsa got an opportunity to study in Canada; but when her mother was later taken ill seriously, her father said he could no longer afford to subsidise her expenses abroad and asked her to quit. And yet, Elsa managed to carry on studying through a bank loan. She did, however, change her major to accounting, a subject with better job prospects. The June-Fourth incident in Beijing in 1989 broke out while she was in Canada, where there were few reports in the media. Elsa joined protests in Toronto but did not retain much of an impression of them. After graduation she worked in Canada and the US, where she got her accountant's licence. This professional qualification allowed her to return eventually to Hong Kong.

Elsa had lost touch with her friends from the Federation of Students until she came back to Hong Kong in 1999. When she saw them again, what stuck in her memory was this picture: "I brought up June-Fourth only to be scolded by my friends, who asked that I let bygones be bygones. On second thoughts, though, I wondered why I should be so persistent when what had happened was in the distant past." In Hong Kong, Elsa never attended the annual June-Fourth candlelight vigil. She imagined she must have become "unpatriotic" because of June-Fourth. "This incident has left me utterly perplexed. I wanted to escape, not willing to face it or remember it."

However, during the anti-Article 23 demonstration in 2003, Elsa took an active part. "From then on, I joined the protest every year for the July 1 march. Usually, I would leave before the crowd reached the destination for fear of the expected congestion." At that time, many Hongkongers would accept that peaceful demonstration was good enough: that the *'wo lei fei'* peaceful protesters were rendering their support to the cause in good faith.

In the summer of 2014, the heat of the Umbrella Movement had a sweeping impact throughout Hong Kong. Elsa was not in town at the time, being on a business trip to Canada. "Night and day while in Canada, I was glued to the Chinese-language news channels and followed the reports in *Apple Daily* [a local newspaper popular for its pro-democracy stance]." Upon return to Hong Kong, she visited the occupied site on Harcourt Road with her younger sister but felt no real impetus to take part in the occupation.

---

1   *Tong-lau* in Cantonese means, literally, a building in the Chinese style, as distinguished from those built in the Western style. The earliest *tong-lau* appeared in Hong Kong and other south China cities in the late 19th century, and they were built up to the 1960s. They could be up to eight floors, without lifts.

2   It All Began with Protecting Our Kids

What caused Elsa to take on a path that changed her destiny completely was the *Protect Our Kids* (POK) campaign. It was 27 July 2019, she remembered, a week after the infamous 7.21 Incident of the White-T-Shirt attackers in Yuen Long, where someone had earlier called for a protest the next day. It was going to be a march in the absence of the police's "Letter of No Objection". Just as Elsa was hesitating whether to join the march, she found a handbill from *Protect Our Kids* she had got earlier. "I hadn't known about the group before; but at that moment the very words 'Protect Our Kids' struck me head on." She had always wanted to "connect" with the young people and was frustrated about the lack of channels. She even thought of visiting the "Lennon Walls" in all eighteen districts of Hong Kong to look for an opportunity to chat with youngsters, but she had never put this thought into action. On 28 July she wanted to join the march with her friends, though she was afraid of the white-T-shirt men and the triad gangs in that area. Finally, she decided to follow the guidelines on the handbill and arrived at the Yuen Long MTR Station for the *Protect Our Kids* gathering.

This was the first time she had taken part in a *Protect Our Kids* activity. She was surprised by its sheer scale. "Almost two hundred people came to gather there, and we were divided into twenty teams. As I had no idea what to do, I followed the team leader's instructions. I felt strange at the time: how come everyone was in 'full gear', and I was totally unprepared."

As they put on their "gear", they were split into the Red Van and the Green Van[2] teams. When they were all set to go, Elsa's eyes were wide open. "The Red Van is despatched to the frontline, while the Green Van is more circumspect. Those who prefer to follow the rules would stay with the Green Van." She said with a smile that the first thing she opted for was to join the Green Van. Everyone in that team wore a green ribbon as a sign. "This would be my first experience. I did not do anything there. I just followed the team with a social worker into a shopping mall. Suddenly, the police appeared out of the blue, all set to fire their tear gas, and so I popped into the metro and left the spot."

Even though the initiators of *Protect Our Kids* were all church preachers and a third of the participants have religious faith, Elsa said she was not a Christian. At the end of every briefing session, they would pray for all who would take part

---

2   The Red Van and Green Van is a colloquial expression in Hong Kong public transport, referring to red and green minibuses. The red ones usually go a longer distance, while green ones follow shorter local routes. Of course, the term in the context here has a different meaning, referring to the risk associated with the operation.

in the activities that evening. She got through the first day not knowing exactly what was going on but continued to participate in activities afterwards. Elsa had the habit of jotting down detailed notes on each event and shared them with her friends who were concerned about what was going on in the streets, to enable them to understand the situation better. "My friends who read them were very touched and hoped I'd continue making these notes and keep them properly informed." Elsa's drive to write was reinforced as the records she made got recognised. "Each time, I tried my best to put down what happened and my feelings about them, before I circulated the notes around the group." After reading her notes, a few girls said they were touched and approached Elsa privately, offering to donate money and requesting that she help to buy supplies for the frontline. "But I was confused: some said they needed 'pig-mouths' [gas masks], but others said they'd already got too many and preferred goggles. I didn't have the means of getting hold of such supplies and was confused about what they really needed." In the end, she passed the money to the *Protect Our Kids* initiators so that they could purchase the necessary supplies.

After the July 28 event, Elsa took part again in the march on 3 August in the Yaumatei/Tsim Sha Tsui/Mongkok area. Not many people were there with the *Protect Our Kids* group, which gathered at the MacPherson Stadium, so she was "upgraded" from the Green Van to the Red Van team. Though she was pleased about the arrangement, she was still very scared. "I hadn't figured out my own inclinations at the time." Confrontation took place first on Austin Road that day and the few blocks nearby were sealed off. Black-clad protesters set up roadblocks at the site, where about 300 policemen were in sight. The group of elderly people to which she belonged put themselves in between the two opposing camps.

In the beginning, they sent someone to ask the black-clad protesters on the frontline whether they would let the volunteers from *Protect Our Kids* stand in the middle to form some sort of divider, Elsa said. The black-clad youth had all along rejected their suggestion, until one of their team leaders, a schoolteacher, convinced them. On the six-lane road, about forty volunteers now stood in the middle, forming themselves into two human chains. As they saw the police suddenly put on their gear, Elsa stood there trembling. "Our own setup was pretty basic. All we had were a helmet, a pair of goggles and a 'single-pig-mouth' [single-canister gas mask]. And as I was putting them on, my legs started to give way."

At this moment, a few youngsters popped up from nowhere and kneeled before a male volunteer in the human chain, urging all the *Protect Our Kids* volunteers to leave the site. "It turned out that they had received messages about police making advances in full gear on that day. Fearing that we might be injured, they went down on their knees to beg us to leave." The male volunteer could not hold back his tears before the young people who were down on their knees. One after one, the black-clad pulled each person in the human chain away from the site until all the *Protect Our Kids* volunteers had gone. Soon afterwards, the police made their advance and opened fire.

In the meantime, the team leader dragged Elsa aside and told her not to hinder the youngsters in action. And then a round of tear gas was fired. Elsa ran away to escape the smoke, and along the way she tried to alert residents on both sides of the street to shut their windows. Soon she found herself in Mongkok and found her way out from there. "I only learnt later that to make sure everyone was safe, all my team members were looking for me. And yet, this kind of team spirit was entirely absent in me [at that time]: driven by fear, I only knew that I must run away from the tear gas to save myself."

3   First Successful Mediation

With the experience of the first two events, Elsa became better adapted to the pace and rhythm of the *Protect Our Kids* team. Group members had developed greater mutual understanding and frequently acted together. Thereafter, demonstrations began to sprout in many local districts. On 5 August, the team chose to gather at Sha Tin. Members then dispersed themselves into various other districts according to their own choice. Once, Elsa was with a team of seven heading to support protesters in Tin Shui Wai. Conflict occurred in a narrow street where residents were throwing stuff from their buildings at the police down below. "Our team leader went with another social worker teammate to try and mediate between the residents and the police, hoping to resolve the conflict." There was no hope whatsoever for dialogue between the police and the residents; the only chance to solve the crisis lay with an external third party. "So, our team leader managed to convey the police's request and promise to the residents: if the residents living on the lower levels and upper levels would all stop throwing objects, the police would also withhold firing their tear gas."

The team leader then spoke with the residents on the site. Having accepted the message, the residents stopped throwing objects down at the police, though they were still too angry to stop shouting. The police had also restrained themselves somewhat; dozens of them gradually moved back to near the footbridge, where they then took off in their vans. A female social worker of the *Protect Our Kids* team applauded when she saw the police retreating, only to be sneered at and scolded by the residents there. "Some remarked that more than seventy young people and protesters were arrested that morning. The youngest among them was only 13 years old. And so, there was nothing to applaud even as the police had eventually left." Elsa had sympathy for the social worker, who was blamed and scolded by the residents for her positive reaction after resolving the crisis at hand. Elsa went over to comfort her. "We also reflected on the incident in our meeting and concluded that neither side had tried to consider the situation from the others' perspectives. We need to deliberate more in future on how we should respond."

4   Building Team Spirit and Rapport

Elsa and her team operated like a local fire brigade – they would go wherever "fire" broke out. The tension between the citizens and the police was high; they were so antagonistic to each other that no communication seemed possible. In the afternoon that same day, there was a blockade formed by protesters around a police station, and the *Protect Our Kids* team went there. According to Elsa, "Many parents had gathered at the site to find out from the station if their children had been arrested in the protest that morning, but to no avail. The police ignored their enquiries." With the *Protect Our Kids*'s mediation efforts, however, the police eventually agreed to pass on to the team a name list of those arrested. Through mediation by the team, the protesters also agreed to "ceasefire" temporarily. "The experience of this incident left a deep impression, for I got to run across roadblocks and rail tracks alongside the young people. In turn, they helped me move all the stuff blocking the way through. And I also learnt to report regularly to my team leader my location and safety."

After several rounds of action, Elsa explained, the team's mode of communication improved. For instance, at the start of an action, members would login an *app* (application, i.e., software programme) on mobile phones, through which a team leader could "call" each teammate on the common platform. Other leaders would receive the same message and maintain mutual communication. On-site communication was supplemented with the use of walkie-talkies. In late September, they got support from a kind of "sentry" watch. A group of young women would keep watch near a police station to monitor the movement of police vans. "When police vans drove out of the station, they would inform us of the number of vehicles despatched and the direction they went. Once the team leaders got the information, they would pass this on to the black-clad protesters at the frontline."

Basically, the *Protect Our Kids* volunteers were divided into teams of seven to ten people. If a particular team had no leader, the number of members in it would be increased accordingly. "Not anyone could be a leader. Team leadership was usually taken up by social workers or somebody with relevant experience. I was not someone eligible, to be sure. I knew that I couldn't run fast, and I didn't have the experience or skill for prompt on-site reactions. So, what I did best was to follow the moves of core members." In addition, members had to follow basic rules. For instance, to ensure full concentration during action, there should be no chanting of slogans and no use of mobile phones. Face masks were not worn.

With experience, Elsa learnt how to better prepare herself for action. Gradually, the rapport with her fellow teammates improved. "I learnt once, quite by accident, that my team leader often did laundry all alone late at night in a self-help laundromat, cleaning all the yellow vests we wore on the streets. From then on, I brought home after each action a few dozen yellow vests to wash. I thought this would help." Before each action, Elsa would also take some individually packed saline solution, disinfectants, and first aid supplies in her backpack. When an action took place in the morning, she would thoughtfully bring along sandwiches and packed drinks. "Often members could only find time to eat their first meal in the afternoon. So, I would carry a big bag, like Lam Ah-Chen,[3] full of everything needed." She laughed when she described how she got onto the bus with her extra-large backpack, making a comical scene.

5   The Single 'Pig-Mouth' Upgraded

Aside from preparation for action, Elsa also experienced gradual change psychologically. August 17 was the day she put on her first full gear. This took place near the Prince Edward Police Station, where Elsa's team found themselves at the confrontation between the anti-riot squad and the protesters. They had followed the protesters from Hung Hom to Prince Edward. At the time the police were in full gear, and Elsa's team leader gave a signal for members to put on theirs. "My hands and legs couldn't stop shaking on the spot; I felt my legs were so weak as to give out. Then someone passing by alerted me to my broken goggles. She took one quickly from her supply bag and gave it to me for replacement."

---

3   Lam Ah-Chen is a fictional character in the 1982 Hong Kong-made comedy *Plain Jane to the Rescue*. The protagonist Jenny Lam Ah-Chen (played by Josephine Siao) is a woman in ordinary clothes, wearing a pair of thick glasses for short-sightedness, and always carries with her a huge bag of stuff. She is straightforward and funny. Sometimes she behaves a bit awkwardly, but she has a strong sense of justice. She remains a popular character with the local audience.

Another remarkable day was when Elsa's gear got upgraded from a "single pig-mouth" to a "dual pig-mouth" (i.e., gas mask with dual canisters). "It was in early October," she said with a touch of emotion, "when I got blessed by six guardian angels on one single day." Assigned to keep watch in Tsim Sha Tsui, she was following the wave of protesters to Yaumatei. This was when they met the anti-riot squad. "We ran and ran, each time with the squad drawing closer. I ran until I was totally exhausted. The record I kept indicated I had taken 20,000 to 30,000 steps at each go, and we had run for hours non-stop that day."

She remembered that 82-year-old Uncle Wong[4] was with her that day. Amazingly, the old gentleman never fell off the team. "Uncle Wong was unbelievably tough! He went with the youngsters all the way from Tsim Sha Tsui East to Caritas Hospital[5] and was pursued all the way by the media. Wearing the yellow reflective vest, Elsa paused at times to help translate what Uncle Wong had to say in response to media questions. "We did quite a few interviews, including for the foreign press from Germany and Czechia, among others. They wanted to take photos, so we needed to stop a bit each time after Uncle Wong's short replies." Following each such interruption, they had to make a greater effort to get back in line with the protest march. "My legs ached so very much that day, so very painful!"

6   Tears on the Battlefield

The team leader was suddenly informed that conflicts had broken out somewhere ahead of them, near Mongkok, where tear gas was fired. In the group there were several other elderly people apart from Uncle Wong. They were too exhausted to reach the protest scene. "Even the more energetic elders were not able to catch up. Because of the pain in my leg, I couldn't run anymore." Just as Elsa was about to put on her gear, she was struck by a huge wave of smoke. "The tear gas being deployed at the time was China-made. It went right into my lungs, and my throat and mouth swelled instantaneously. Filled with a mouthful of smoke, I could not utter a single word. I got very nervous. The more I became anxious about not being able to talk, the more I felt the pain in my throat and eyes. I wanted to catch up with my team leader to say I needed

---

4   Uncle Wong, a member of *Protect Our Kids*, was over eighty years of age. In the New Year march of 2020, he was arrested by the police in Causeway Bay. On the day, a total of 400 people were arrested, including 6 members of POK.

5   Approximately 6 km.

to step aside to rinse my eyes and put on my gear, but I could hardly even move to do so."

As the tear gas smoke continued to spread, Elsa escaped into an alley and lost touch with the team. She could hardly breathe. "I suddenly heard someone call my name. He was a teammate and his emergence at that point was practically angelic!" Elsa was carrying a lot of supplies in her bag, but in her disorientated state, she got totally confused and forgot all about self-help. At this point, the teammate rinsed her eyes out with water. She calmed down a bit and was soon able to speak. She cleaned up at a washroom in a nearby hotel and there got a call from her team leader. When she stepped out of the hotel, the sentinel he sent along was waiting for her at the entrance to offer help.

> I kept meeting my guardian angels. Two teammates helped clean my eyes and face, and on the way two youngsters took care of me as they passed by. They said my single-pig-mouth mask was not good enough and offered to give me a dual-pig-mouth instead.

Elsa declined their offer firmly, saying that she was not someone at the frontline and would not want to use up the supplies unnecessarily.

> But the two youngsters insisted that I take the mask they handed me. Six people joined in the effort to persuade me to accept it until I really could not decline anymore. I was very touched when I put on the dual-pig-mouth gas mask.

In the end, the "angels" led her to cross the roadblocks to find her team in the battlefield. "It was like looking for your lost family across thousands of miles."

Later, when she sat down to eat in Mongkok, something else unforgettable happened to her. In the restaurant, three teenagers of about fourteen, fifteen years of age were staring at her across the tables. At this point, Elsa recalled her team leader's advice: "He said, should we come across young female protesters at the frontline, we would try our best to ask them not to go all the way to the front as that would be especially dangerous for young girls."

So, when Elsa caught sight of the young girls staring at her in the restaurant, she walked right up to them, intending to tell them to be careful. But before she could speak all the girls broke into tears. "They said every time they saw people like us – elderly volunteers in yellow vests, or Uncle Wong with his dedicated efforts, they could not help themselves but break down into tears." The young girls said that they could not understand why things had come to where they were. They looked very perplexed trying to figure out why even retired elderly people felt they had to go to the frontline. They felt so lost and so sad. Elsa gave each of them a hug and said comforting words to soothe their young souls, rounding up with the reminder for them to take good care of themselves. "I said to them, someday we would be able to take our masks off and meet each other '*under the pot*'."[6]

The yellow reflective vests worn by the *Protect Our Kids* volunteers had left a deep impression on those staying at protest sites. They provided a sense of reassurance for many young protesters, some of whom also sought relief for their emotional outbursts at the frontline. Elsa recalled one incident at New Town Plaza in Sha Tin. A young man suddenly came up to a male member of the team and cried his eyes out right in front of him.

On another occasion in early October, there was a huge crowd of protesters, which the team leader described as a massive "exodus", yet without the police's "Letter of No Objection" for the demonstration. The protesters soon ran into two water cannon vehicles coming out from Causeway Bay to chase the crowd into Wanchai Market. People were running in panic and in every direction, as the vehicles pushed forward. *Protect Our Kids* volunteers and a group of youngsters made their way up to Bowen Road. As they ran, people put on their gear when they were midway up the hill. Making sure the police were not behind them, everyone paused to catch a breath. At this point a young man of about 22 or 23 years of age came up to the team and bowed to each one of the members. Elsa was curious:

> Usually, they would nod to us to express gratitude from a distance. This young man's initiative did surprise me. After bowing and thanking us, he burst into tears and could not calm down for some time. He said he would have been arrested earlier were it not for our intervention. He was immensely touched by our help, which was why he couldn't restrain himself emotionally when he saw us face-to-face just now.

Elsa had been transformed gradually but completely. She was no longer the person whose legs started shaking every time she put on her protective gear.

---

6 "Meet one another under the pot" was a popular and somewhat romantic expression of encouragement in the Anti-ELAB Movement. "*Under the pot*" refers to the once legal demonstration area under the Council Chamber of the Legislative Council building, as it is shaped like a rice-pot from the outside. The protesters looked forward to a time when Hong Kong would become open and democratic, when they could all celebrate and meet one another in the demonstration area where they had met before, with no need to hide their faces behind masks.

Now she walked fearlessly into the warzone. What had become indelible experiences of her life, however, were the incidents on the campuses of the Chinese University and the Polytechnic University. "In the dozens of events I had joined, not one could compare to the Chinese University incident. So many rounds of tear gas were fired by the police at machine-gun speed and frequency. So many people got injured; no one could tell what the actual number was."

7   The Battle of the Chinese University

The battle of the Chinese University Bridge No. 2 took place on 11 November 2019. When Elsa arrived at the campus with the *Protect Our Kids* team, the police and the protesters were already confronting each other there. The Vice Chancellor of the University had tried to negotiate with the police, but the tension had not eased. As the team approached the slope near the bridge, they saw a few youngsters on guard with their umbrellas. The leader asked Elsa and another member to talk to them and see what they had in mind. The other member, herself a mother, started up a conversation. She said she had got a doctor's appointment for having coughed up blood the day before, but still decided to come as she learnt about the severe situation at Bridge No. 2. She wanted to see for herself that the young people were safe. Elsa advised the youngsters not to take offensive action but stay calm and patient while gauging how the situation might evolve.

> We could only ask them not to provoke the police, but since they had set up their defences, it was hard to persuade anyone to leave. As our team leader kept reminding us, the young people all had their own independent thoughts. Hence, we should never ask them to leave or push them into taking any course of action. We could only remind them to take caution in everything.

There were flames everywhere at Bridge No. 2. At the time, it would have been futile to try and do anything. Still, the leader teamed up with Elsa and another member, a mother herself, to go and talk to the police, thinking that communication with two women on the side might go easier with the commander. That trick had worked in the past, but not this time. Bridge No. 2 was a total warzone. "The police acted fiercely, not permitting us to cross the road even though we showed no sign of doing any harm." In the end, before they could get in touch with the commander, the three of them were stopped at police gunpoint and could only turn back to the youngsters' defence line.

No sooner had they turned around did the police open fire. Elsa's group put on their gear right away.

> Firing continued non-stop within the 50-metre area around us, didn't stop even for a moment! This was the first time I had experienced such an aggressive act with the guns thundering, amid the dozens of events I had witnessed. You had no idea what they were shooting either: tear gas, pepper-spray pellets, anything. You only knew it wouldn't stop.

In the dense smoke, Elsa could not see a thing, but she was not afraid. Her legs no longer shook, though she felt the severe pain on her skin where it was not covered by the face mask and goggles. Along with two journalists, they hid themselves in a bush to cut down the chance of being hit. They anticipated that the police would launch a massive arrest after those rounds of firing. "When that happened, we were prepared to grab whoever we could, to help save even just one more youngster."

No one had expected that after an hour of shooting the police had little intention of ceasing fire. "From the sides, we knelt low and saw first aid volunteers move the injured to level ground further away. There was nothing we could do, except feeling anxious." Even though she kept her protective gear tight, Elsa said the visibility through her smoked goggles was reduced to almost 1/10. "You could hardly see anything." Many teammates had run to other spots to escape the suffocating smoke. Elsa got herself into a small bungalow which was only 70 or 80 metres away from the police. "One of the rooms was not locked, so I just got in. I saw a lot of injured people lying down inside, some rather seriously injured." Elsa remembered what it was like inside the room.

> Even though all the windows were closed, the smell of tear gas had penetrated inside. The second I took off my goggles, my eyes started to burn with excruciating pain, and I had to reluctantly cover my face with water.

This bungalow turned out to be an office of graduate students, with six or seven work desks in it. Elsa hid under a desk to rinse her eyes and saw numerous first-aiders coming in and out, with about ten students hiding indoors.

As Elsa came in to take shelter, the firing outside had subsided a bit. But then they heard the anti-riot squad searching the area outside the office, so everyone inside did not dare to make any noise and Elsa restrained herself from coughing. As she glimpsed from the sides of the window, she saw two *Protect Our Kids* members pass by, so she opened the door cautiously to let them in. One of them was the mother-volunteer she had worked with earlier. She was holding two baskets of bottled distilled water for rescue purposes when an anti-riot policeman shouted at her, "Don't move!" He pointed his gun at her, asking her to open the door for the squad to enter. At this moment, the mother cried, "Don't shoot! Don't shoot." She figured that when the police found that she was not a young person, they would just let her go without pushing for their search. When the police left, she could bring the water in for rinsing the eyes and wounds of the injured people there.

There were many other stories on the day at Bridge No. 2. Elsa felt she must keep a record of them. Amid the ongoing flames and chaos, a young-ster, apparently a university student, tried to approach the police holding an electric saw which was initially used to cut tree branches for setting up road-blocks. Now that the saw was fetched by the young man, the situation did not look good. Under those chaotic circumstances, nobody had paid attention to his strange behaviour until the team leader cried out, "Stop him!" One team member jumped over the fence deftly towards him, while Elsa also caught up from behind, and together, they managed to restrain him. Elsa recalled that the young man was still very agitated when they tried to calm him down and talk with him. To prevent his appearance from being exposed to the camera, Elsa opened an umbrella swiftly to cover him.

A female teammate held the young man's hand and patted his shoulders to comfort him. Finally, he was willing to turn off the electric saw, and spoke in agony, "I want to die! My whole family should die!" We learnt later that his family were all police and he had not gone home for a long time. He said he no longer had a home. "The young man said his family had caused harm to so many *sau zuks* [brothers and sisters]. He felt guilty and wanted to make good with his death." Our teammates talked to him until he calmed down and prom-ised not to do anything silly again. Though still concerned about him, they had to let him go.

Another young girl was crying as she walked through the ruins outside, look-ing around anxiously in all directions. She had earlier helped bring a young man shot by a sponge grenade in the chest to the medical room for attention. She was eager to look around to find him and to see how he was. Different people helped several times to spread the message around, until it was finally confirmed that a medical student had attended to the case. "We learnt later that Sung Jao Yiu[7] had led a group of medical students to take on the rescue work. Some injured persons were sent to another place for treatment." This

---

7   Professor Joseph Sung Jao Yiu was the former Vice-Chancellor of The Chinese University of Hong Kong. He was a faculty member of the Faculty of Medicine.

"another place", according to Elsa, was secretive. This was indicative of the dreadful atmosphere clouded with suspicion at the Chinese University campus that day.

> One of our members helped to transport an injured woman for treatment somewhere, not to the hospital, but to 'another place' through a meandering route by ensuring they were not followed on the way. She was shot in her leg and surgery had to be done. The cost for the medical treatment amounted to sixty thousand dollars.

Elsa said the doctor in charge volunteered for the operation, but the equipment and medication had to be paid. "Fees were covered by a fund, so the injured did not need to pay."

8   The Battle of the Polytechnic University

Hong Kong never had a chance to recuperate from the trauma of the Chinese University conflict. Immediately after that, people had to face yet an even more atrocious event at the Polytechnic University (PolyU). Elsa and the *Protect Our Kids* volunteers soon moved to the battlefield on another campus, not knowing what kind of destiny or encounter lay ahead. Even in retrospect, Elsa could not shake off the sense of weariness from her face. "During the two days at PolyU, I practically had no sleep. I spent the next two days at the police station, sleepless. With only about five or six hours of sleep in four days, I was hollowed out in total fatigue."

In the afternoon of 17 November, about five or six teams headed toward PolyU to render support. Elsa recalled, "Once we were on site at the campus, we realised that the situation outside was dangerous, and confrontation very intense. So, we did not go out." In the evening, rumours had it that anyone leaving the campus after eight o'clock would be charged with rioting. Nobody could confirm the truthfulness of the message. Hence, the teams stayed put and did nothing. Rumours kept spreading during that time. Elsa said she learnt that a group of people were arrested just as they stepped out of the campus. "We believed this was a trap."

At night, they had thought about leaving but could not find a way out. Hesitant and uncertain about everything, they could only leave their names and personal details with the *daai toi* (literally the centre stage, but it refers to *Protect Our Kids'* central monitoring platform here), hoping that teammates outside could get to know their condition inside. "It was estimated that at least a thousand people were inside PolyU that night."

After midnight, all the *Protect Our Kids* volunteers were exhausted and were taking a rest. Suddenly, the first-aiders came to wake them up and ask them to join their rescue. "Normally, there were plenty of first-aiders around and we would not take part in their work. But this time there were too many injured people to take care of and we had to help." The first-aiders only briefly outlined how they separated the severely injured from those less so. Their teammates had to take care of the latter as best they could. What they did was to help rinse and clean the injured or apply ointment, as the case might require. "There was truly 'no main stage' nobody was commanding. The injured were mostly male, but female teammates also helped to clean their wounds." Many people had been hit by the blue toxic spray or tear gas, which affected the skin extensively, causing tremendous pain. One youngster had been hit three times by the water cannon. Every time he came in to have his body washed, he would return right away to the warzone afterwards, mumbling, "Must go and save our brothers!"

> I can't even describe the kind of pain he experienced. I had asked him not to go back there, but he always retorted: 'Brothers out there cannot sustain the defence. We are short of manpower.'

Elsa admitted that they were all in tears as they hastened to rinse his body. Seeing that so many people had given up their future to make such fearless commitments, she was deeply touched and felt that she was also prepared to give whatever she could.

And then people got hungry. *Protect Our Kids* volunteers thought they could help to cook, so they shifted to 'battle' in the kitchen. "Stepping into Maxim's Cafeteria [on the campus], we found the floor covered in broken glass as the restaurant had earlier been 'refurbished'[8] by protesters. Dishes were thrown about, and tables had toppled on the floor."

---

8 For 'refurbish', see footnote 8, Chap 8 Maxim's was targeted because of the words said by Annie Wu Shuk-ching, the eldest daughter of Maxim's founder James Tak Wu, during the Movement. Annie Wu was a prominent businesswoman with huge investments in China, and a member of the Standing Committee of the Political Consultative Conference in China. She condemned the Anti-ELAB Movement early on, and said that she gave up on the younger generation of Hong Kong, accusing them of being "brainwashed". She also put pressure on the Chinese Foundation Secondary School, which she founded in 2000, to punish students who had come out to support the movement.

Elsa took cardboard cartons to organise any usable supplies and cleared the rubbish on the floor so that people could rest there. "Actually, I felt so weak myself, feeling that my two legs were no longer mine." She said frankly that there were no leaders in PolyU then. Indeed, the *Protect Our Kids* folks functioned as an organised support team. "In times like that, there could no longer be any leaders. Each one of us had to apply oneself to whatever seemed necessary and feasible."

Elsa had come to admire a teammate of *Protect Our Kids*, a retiree in her seventies. "She took part every time alongside her son, a team leader. She just followed him and was out at the frontline every time." She bought in a massive amount of supplies, and for pig-mouth masks alone, she got over a hundred of them. "In every action she brought a lot of supplies to deliver to team members. She put in both money and effort. In the end, she and I were arrested and detained together at the police station." When many people on PolyU campus got hungry at midnight, this retired lady went into the snack counter and cooked some simple food. "She busied herself at the kitchenette for a couple of hours. Whoever was hungry would go in to get fed, as she cooked continuously to provide food for everybody." Elsa said she had initially wanted to help in some way but felt just too tired to give her a hand. "I got angry with myself just for that!"

Elsa used to not care so much about the outside world, and then she used to find her legs giving way whenever she had to put on her protective gear in the field. In the end, she was arrested in the PolyU battlefield. "Frankly, I was psychologically prepared for that. So, when I was arrested, I felt quite calm." But her friends were very worried and hurried to find lawyers for her. As she held a foreign passport, they also tried to contact the embassy to see if they could offer any help. Elsa recalled that as they were setting off to PolyU earlier that day, the team leader had said there was an 80% to 90% chance of getting arrested this time. He asked teammates to assess their own situation and capacity to bear the consequences and said anyone could opt out at any time. "But nobody raised a hand to opt out. However, we had thought that the charge would be obstruction of police work or illegal assembly. No one had expected that we would be charged with rioting eventually."

Over forty members of the *Protect Our Kids* team were arrested in the end. Elsa was detained for 43 hours. "The place [at the police station] was like a parking lot. The police marked off an area of not more than a hundred square feet to lock up over a hundred women there. Next to it was a similar area marked off for men, where a hundred or so were detained." They sat on the rugged cement floor, which was very uncomfortable. But the retired old lady took it easy, eating and sleeping as normal. "She finished off an awful lunchbox without leaving a single grain of rice in it. It's incredible how she, once a senior administrator, could evolve into this woman I saw before me!"

9   Walking Together to the End

Elsa had come all this way. When she was eventually arrested and charged, how did she feel? What was in her mind? After some deliberation, she said,

> Some friends of mine had asked me the same question. How would a volunteer who just wanted to protect the kids end up becoming a protester who got arrested? I replied that I have never changed.

Once she was arrested, she felt like she could eventually take the yellow vest off, put aside the rules which she had to follow, and put down her baggage, physical or otherwise. She could now sit down in peace once again, and have a good chat with the young people, taking on another role and way of dialogue, to understand them, and to observe the evolvement of the entire Movement, its twists and turns.

"Since the very beginning, we have always stood on the side of the young people. They have chosen to protest in this time of ours, and we have chosen to protect them." Elsa admitted that in the early phase of the Movement, there were many things she could not accept at all.

> I believe the public had the same reaction. For instance, protesters' behaviours like confronting the police head-on. But if we understand the root cause and origin of the movement, we can understand them better, even if we cannot agree with all they did.

She said everyone in the whole team had been learning throughout the process, putting oneself constantly in the shoes of the young people. "If you have children capable of independent thinking, you won't be able to change them one way or another. At the same time, if the kids also know that they need to bear the responsibility in future for what they have done, that is good enough. They have chosen their way, and we will back them up to the end."

CHAPTER 13

Lessons from Hong Kong

1 The Changed Face of Hong Kong

The COVID-19 pandemic set in shortly after the Chinese New Year in spring 2020, spreading, as it did, from the Chinese city of Wuhan to Hong Kong and to all over the world. Lockdown measures followed rapidly, complete with restrictions on public gathering and digital checks for entry to various public places. These measures, coupled with harsh police clampdown on public protests, and most importantly, the National Security Law (NSL), threw a shroud of silence and terror all over Hong Kong. Particularly noticeable was the NSL, which was passed with record-breaking speed in the Standing Committee of the National People's Congress in Beijing and was put into force on 1 July 2020. Despite drastic changes it would bring to society, the contents were unknown to anyone in Hong Kong before that date, and any form of deliberation or input from Hong Kong inhabitants was out of the question.

At the time of writing, in the summer of 2022, Hong Kong is a completely different place. Many political commentators, particularly those who have joined the exodus leaving the territory, often refer sardonically to the "New Hong Kong", or even "South Shenzhen", degrading the once robust, international city to a second-tier mainland border town.

Indeed, one sees clear signs of change everywhere. For example, after Xi Jinping officiated and gave a short speech at the swearing-in ceremony of the new Chief Executive on 1 July 2022, a rapid succession of classes or seminars followed immediately, purportedly trying to "learn the important spirit behind Chairman Xi's speech". Conducting "learning classes/seminars" after a leader made a speech, or after a new policy document was issued, is a time-worn practice in Communist China as well as CCP organs and pro-Beijing institutions in Hong Kong, but this time, this practice spread widely, encompassing political parties, business councils, government officials, and even professional groups. Tik Chi-yuen, the only so-called "non-pro-Establishment" Legislative Councillor after the Legislative Council election mechanism was "perfected" (CCP-speak, meaning to ensure that dissenting voices would not appear) in 2021, admitted that these "learning classes" had been rare in Hong Kong. He himself was still adjusting to it, but he "would still have his own views". Ivan Choy Chi-keung, a rare political scientist and academic who still agreed to be interviewed by the press after NSL, said that such learning classes constituted an installation of a mainland "political learning" culture in Hong Kong. "This is a time-honed practice in the mainland, ... now as we enter a new era, as politics in Hong Kong is 'mainlandised', this kind of political culture is transmitted to Hong Kong."[1]

What happened is, of course, not only a transmission of mainland political culture to Hong Kong. Social institutions are under severe threat too.

1.1 *The Judicial System*

The anachronistic Public Order Ordinance of the colonial era was resuscitated in the 2010s to bring charges against public protests. The most prominent one was the trial and conviction of nine activists, in April 2019, who were involved in the "Occupy Central" movement (tied to the Umbrella Movement) of 2014.[2] This caused a local and international uproar because the Umbrella Movement had earlier attracted international attention and was a worldwide exemplar of peaceful protest. Then, in 2020, sedition charges were brought against an outspoken pro-democracy activist, Tam Tak-chi, who had uttered verbal attacks on the government shortly after the proclamation of the National Security Law. He was soon followed by others who had either published, displayed posters, or posted social media messages to express dissent.[3] Charges and convictions now do not rest on whether there was incitement of immediate violence, as is the international standard. Words alone are sufficient for indictment. This is a big step taken to silence criticisms of the government or of the Chinese state.

A more destructive attack on the rule of law was the National Security Law (NSL). Its ruinous effects on the rule of law were prominently featured in a report issued by the United Nations Human Rights Committee on 27 July 2022 (UN Human Rights Committee, 2022). It notes that the NSL prevails over local laws when in conflict and is thus capable of overriding fundamental rights and freedoms protected by the International Covenant on Civil and Political Rights (ICCPR), of which Hong Kong is a co-signatory. The Committee observes that "the overly broad interpretation of and arbitrary application of the Law" (UN Human Rights Committee, 2022, para. 12) has led to the arrests of over 200

---

1 "Classes to learn Xi's speech popular; Political circles brush up KPI; Avoid talking about entrenched interests", *HK01*, 7 July 2022, https://www.hko1.com/sns/article/789476 (in Chinese, last viewed on 9 Aug 2022).

2 "Nine found guilty in Hong Kong Court of Occupy Central Public Order Charges", Radio Free Asia, 9 Apr 2019. https://www.rfa.org/english/news/china/charges-04092019102223.html, (last viewed 20 Aug 2022).

3 "Hong Kong's sedition law is back", *The Diplomat*, 3 Sept 2021, https://thediplomat.com/2021/09/hong-kongs-sedition-law-is-back/, (last viewed 3 Sept 2021).

persons since 2020, including 12 children, with 44 convictions of 12 people not falling within the four categories of offences in the Law. The NSL is also accused of undermining basic legal principles. Among other things, the lack of clarity on "national security" and on what constitutes a crime under the Law undermines the principle of legal certainty. Then, the excessive power of the Chief Executive and other measures provided for in the Law undermines the independence of judiciary and procedural safeguards for access to justice and right to a fair trial. There is also a lack of judicial oversight over the extensive investigative powers of the Department for Safeguarding National Security in the police force. Perhaps the greatest worry lies in the provisions that national security cases could be transferred to organs of the Central People's Government for investigation, prosecution, trial, and execution of penalties, while China is not a party to the ICCPR. Afterall, it was the fear of the demolition of the "firewall" between the Hong Kong and the mainland legal systems that had ignited the 2019 protests.

This fear is, unfortunately, well-founded. While transference of cases to the mainland has not yet taken place, the presumption of innocence until proven guilty, hitherto a fundamental tenet of the legal system in Hong Kong, is completely overturned. According to the UN Human Rights Committee Report, "about 74 per cent of persons charged with national security crimes allegedly have been denied bail without proper reasoning and many people have been in pre-trial detention, including 11 children, and some of them are reportedly in pre-trial detention for more than a year" (UN Human Rights Committee, 2022, para. 35c). This follows from a provision in the NSL that bail shall not be granted "unless the judge has sufficient grounds for believing that the criminal suspect or defendant will not continue to commit acts endangering national security."[4] The most notorious case is the arrest and detention of the organisers and participants of the 2020 primary election in the pan-democracy camp. To date, 34 out of the 47 charged have been in detention since 28 February 2021, still awaiting trial. Another such case is the arrest and detention of 6 senior executive and editorial staff of the dissenting newspaper *Apple Daily*. They were arrested after a second raid of the newspaper offices in June 2021 and are still in detention awaiting trial at the time of writing. So are the senior staff of the online news website, *Standnews*.

The NSL has overturned yet another long standing feature of the legal system in Hong Kong: trial by jury. Under the NSL, a case can be tried in the High Court by a panel of designated judges instead of a jury. The first such case of

---

4   Article 42(2) of the National Security Law.

trial in the High Court without jury involved the activist Tong Ying-kit, who was sentenced to 9 years in jail for displaying a banner with "Liberate Hong Kong, Revolution of Our Times". At the time of writing, it was already ruled that two other cases would be tried in the High Court without jury, namely, the 47 persons involved in the primary election case mentioned above, and the founder of *Apple Daily*[5] Jimmy Lai (plus three related companies).

1.2   *The Media and Freedom of Expression*

Independent media, being one of the main targets of the NSL, suffers tremendously. As noted above, the *Apple Daily* was raided and closed in June 2021. Jimmy Lai had his private assets (as well as company assets) frozen, arrested and detained till now. He was since sentenced to a couple of other crimes under the sedition law for protest gatherings, one being the June 4th Vigil in 2020. Public speculation is that he would remain in custody even after he has served these sentences, since the trial for his more serious "crimes" (secession, and collusion with foreign powers etc.) has yet to begin. Then, *Standnews,* a well-subscribed online news website with a pro-democracy editorial position, was raided by the police in December 2021, with its assets frozen and its senior staff arrested and detained. At the same time, the government-funded public broadcasting company, Radio Hong Kong (RTHK), began to phase out programmes that were critical of the government from mid-2020. By 2022, RTHK has lost its previous social standing as an independent broadcaster, and all its programmes that critiqued the government or were high-quality works of investigative journalism are gone Independent publishers, artists and writers are also purged or even arrested, one notorious example being the arrest and pre-trial detention, for over one year at the time of writing, of the founders and executives of the General Union of Speech Therapists for publishing allegedly seditious children's cartoons.[6] In this case, which did not fall under NSL, the Court of Appeal ruled that the accused had to be remanded without bail in any case, since the offence was *related to* national security, so the higher threshold

---

5   "National Security Trial for Hong Kong media mogul Jimmy Lai to proceed without jury – reports", *Hong Kong Free Press,* 17 Aug 2022. https://hongkongfp.com/2022/08/17/natio nal-security-trial-for-hong-kong-media-mogul-jimmy-lai-to-proceed-without-jury-reports/, (last viewed 19 Aug 2022).

6   The 5 speech therapists were subsequently found guilty of sedition and were each sentenced to 19 months in September 2022, after having been remanded in jail for over one year. See "5 Hong Kong speech therapists jailed for 19 months each for sedition over children's books", *Hong Kong Free Press,* 10 Sept 2022. https://hongkongfp.com/2022/09/10/breaking-5-hong -kong-speech-therapists-jailed-for-19-months-each-for-sedition-over-childrens-books/ (last viewed 17 Sept 2022).

for bail also applied.[7] Apart from these, there are also arrests of administrators of various social media platforms from time to time for crimes of sedition or even secession. The chilling effect is keenly felt, so much so that many political commentators either keep quiet or continue their critique only after leaving Hong Kong.

1.3 The Shrinking of Civil Society

The dissolution of the Professional Teachers' Union (PTU) in September 2021, and that of the Confederation of Trade Unions (CTU) a month later sent a clear message to all local as well as overseas observers that the once vibrant civil society is rapidly disintegrating. Founded in 1973, the PTU was the oldest and biggest independent trade union in the history of Hong Kong, and, until its demise, a major support and mouthpiece for the pro-democracy camp. The CTU was founded in 1990, and was the biggest confederation of trade unions, having supported several significant strikes in different trades, most notably, the steel-benders' strike (2007) and the container-terminal strike (2013). Both PTU and CTU were disbanded after a barrage of venomous attacks from mainland and pro-Beijing commentators, this being the usual practice of stamping out groups or individuals who dare to express dissent. Commentators have earlier observed the emergence of many communities or civil society organisations, including new trade unions, towards the end of the 2019 protests, seeing this as more concrete challenges to the entrenched power structure (Lee, 2022; Lee, 2021; Au, 2020). Vines, for example, applauded these efforts as "weaving the protest movement into the fabric of society" (Vines, 2021, p. 194). Sadly, these young, lesser-known groups met the same fate as PTU and CTU, disappearing as the crushing footsteps of the NSL police closed in.

The Hong Kong Alliance in Support of Patriotic Movements in China was raided by the NSL police in September 2021, and its executive members were arrested and detained. They were charged with sedition and subversion of the Chinese state, and were refused bail (the Chairman, Lee Cheuk-yan, and Vice-Chairwoman, Chou Hang-tung, were already in prison for other sedition offences).[8] The Alliance had been organising a yearly candlelight vigil

---

7 "Stringent national security bail threshold applicable to other offences, Hong Kong's top court rules", *Hong Kong Free Press*, 15 Dec 2021, https://hongkongfp.com/2021/12/15/string ent-national-security-bail-threshold-applicable-to-other-offences-hong-kongs-top-court -rules/ (last viewed 19 Aug 2022).

8 Albert Ho Chun-yan was granted bail on stringent terms in the High Court on 22 Aug 2022, after having been refused bail by the District Court a month earlier, when he should have been released after he completed his jail sentence for various convictions related to illegal assembly.

in Victoria Park on Hong Kong Island for 30 years (1990–2020) since the Tiananmen Massacre in 1989. With its demise, Hong Kong is no longer able to host this annual reminder of the shameful and inconvenient memory of the Massacre, which the Beijing powerholders still try desperately to cover up.

1.4   Censorship and CCP Propaganda

Following the crushing of independent media comes naturally censorship in all areas, not only the press. Public libraries removed books that did not comply with national security and so did school libraries (UN Human Rights Committee, 2022, para. 43). Some publishers which had published books on the 2019 Movement were barred from joining the annual Book Fair in July 2022.[9] When one of them organised an independent book fair on his own, the landlord revoked the hiring contract for the venue at the last minute.[10] Writers and artists either left Hong Kong to continue their work, or simply keep quiet. Ordinary people now become very careful when they post entries on social media, rightly so, as national security police arrest and charge people for seditious posting on social media from time to time.

Schools and universities are the most important and convenient targets for CCP propaganda, understandably so, given that teenagers and youths constituted most of the participants in the 2019 Movement. Liberal Studies, previously a compulsory subject on critical thinking for the school-leaving examination, had been repeatedly blamed for misleading young minds, and it is now replaced by a nationalistic programme of Citizenship and Social Development.[11] For this new subject, all students must take mandatory trips to the so-called Greater Bay Area in south Guangdong.[12] The Education Bureau

---

9   "Crowds still flock to Hong Kong's book fair but 'sensitive' topics are absent", *Hong Kong Free Press*, 23 July 2022, https://hongkongfp.com/2022/07/23/crowds-still-flock-to-hong-kongs-book-fair-but-sensitive-topics-are-absent/, (last viewed on 12 Aug 2022).

10   The organiser was Yeung Tze-chun, who lost most of his eyesight in one eye, after having been hit by a tear gas canister in the legal assembly on 12 June 2019. He was later charged and convicted with two counts of illegal assembly and sentenced to a 9-month jail sentence in August 2022. See "Former teacher, Yeung Tze-chun, injured in his right eye, admitted to crime of illegal assembly and jailed for 9 months", RTHK (instant news), 15 Aug 2022. (in Chinese) https://news.rthk.hk/rthk/ch/component/k2/1662515-20220815.htm (last viewed 30 Aug 2022).

11   "Hong Kong University requires students to take 'national security education class'", *Radio Free Asia*, 26 July 2022, see section entitled "A political mission", https://www.rfa.org/english/news/china/national-security-class-07262022111557.html (last viewed 12 Aug 2022).

12   "Hong Kong's Education Bureau releases itineraries for mandatory Citizenship and Social Development trip to mainland China", *Young Post*, 15 July 2022, https://www.scmp.com/yp/discover/news/hong-kong/article/3185298/hong-kongs-education-bureau-releases-itineraries (last viewed 12 Aug 2022).

also distributed "National Security Education" curriculum documents to all primary and secondary schools, advising them on how to incorporate national security education into individual subjects.[13] "Patriotic education" is the keyword, and this comes with all sorts of paraphernalia like regular national flag raising ceremonies,[14] commemoration of Japanese massacre in Nanjing in 1937,[15] etc. National security education is also introduced in universities,[16] and one of these institutions is planning to make a trip to the so-called "Greater Bay Area" in Guangdong mandatory for its students.[17]

From 2020 onwards, Hong Kong has indeed become a different place. This change triggered yet another wave of emigration, following those in mid-1980s and the early 1990s.[18] Viewing these changes from a longer time-perspective,

---

13   Education Bureau Circular No.4/2021, https://www.edb.gov.hk/attachment/en/curricu lum-development/renewal/CM/EDBC21004E.pdf (last viewed on 12 Aug 2022), HKSAR, Education Bureau, 22 April 2021.

14   "All Hong Kong schools must display Chinese national flag, hold weekly flag raising ceremony from next year", Hong Kong Free Press, 12 Oct 2021, https://hongkongfp.com/2021 /10/12/all-hong-kong-schools-must-display-chinese-national-flag-hold-weekly-flag-rais ing-ceremonies-from-next-year/ (last viewed 8 Aug 2022); "Hong Kong marks National Security Education Day with anti-terrorism drills, weapon displays for students as top official urges resolve for defending 'bottom line'" *South China Morning Post*, 15 April 2021, https://www.scmp.com/news/hong-kong/politics/article/3129602/hong-kong-must -show-resolve-defending-bottom-line-national (last viewed 12 Aug 2022); "Hong Kong leader vows to push 'patriotic education' in city's schools to stop being misled", *South China Morning Post*, 10 July 2021.

15   "Education Bureau recommends schools to commemorate victims of Nanjing Massacre on 13th next month", *Headlines*, 22 Nov 2021, https://tinyurl.com/5569ctu3 (in Chinese, last viewed 12 Aug 2022).

16   "HKU makes national security education compulsory for students' graduation", *The Standard*, 25 Jul 2022, https://www.thestandard.com.hk/breaking-news/section/4/192 690/HKU-makes-national-security-education-compulsory-for-students%E2%80%99 -graduation (last viewed 12 Aug 2022).

17   "Education University launches pilot experiential education in Greater Bay Area next year; All undergraduates from 2026 onwards must go on expedition in Greater Bay Area", *Ming Pao*, 27 July 2022, https://tinyurl.com/yc4w3p2s (in Chinese, last viewed 12 Aug 2022).

18   There was a significant decrease of 1.6% in the Hong Kong population in 2022. Government spokesman blamed this on the pandemic restrictions, saying that this would revert once these were lifted. An academic said, however, that this trend would continue, and those who are leaving are mostly young, professional families. See "Decrease of HK population by 1.6%. More than 110,000 people left in a year. Government put the blame on the pandemic. Academic urges directly confronting wave of emigration," *Hong Kong Economic Journal*, 12 Aug 2022, https://tinyurl.com/2p9ykkey (in Chinese, last viewed 19 Sept 2022). It was noted on an internet web news report that emigration figures, which had started as a trickle in

one could see that perhaps all these lamentable changes: undermining of the rule of law, restrictions on the media and all forms of freedom of expression, the destruction of civil society, etc. are inevitable, and that they have been embedded in the non-executable framework in the "One Country Two Systems" early on. One could argue that the different, even unrecognisable face of Hong Kong as it is now would have manifested itself sooner or later, with or without the 2019 protests. Or, one could say that even the 2019 protests were inevitable.

2   The Iron Fist Closing on a Recalcitrant "New, Young Nation"[19]

In her brief but comprehensive discussion of Hong Kong's "decolonisation struggle" against the Chinese global power project, Lee (2022) pointed at "a fundamental contradiction inherent in 'One Country, Two Systems' blueprint, which is an authoritarian party-state and its careerist agents, ruling over a citizenry habituated to a common law tradition of legality and rights" (p. 13). This contradiction inevitably manifested itself time and again in large-scale protests after the 1997 handover, the first spectacular one being the march of half-million people against the introduction of a national security law in line with Article 23 of the Basic Law (Lee, 2022).

2019, now became a steady stream: more than 140,000 people left Hong Kong in the first quarter of 2022. See "Why are so many people leaving Hong Kong?" *GRID*, 30 June 2022. https://www.grid.news/story/global/2022/06/30/why-are-so-many-people-leaving-hong -kong/ (last viewed 19 Sept 2022). Since the implementation of the National Security Law, various English-speaking countries have offered Hong Kong immigrants accessible ways of applying for citizenship. These include: the British National (Overseas) Visa Programme, Canada open work permit programme for recent graduates and Canada permanent residence pathway for in-Canada Hong Kong residents, and Australia permanent residence programme for in-Australia Hong Kong residents. See "A Guide to Global Immigration Pathways for Hong Kong Residents", *MONDAQ*, 10 Mar 2022, https://www.mondaq.com/ hongkong/work-visas/1170442/a-guide-to-global-immigration-pathways-for-hong-kong -residents (last viewed 19 Sept 2022). Yet another emigration destination is Taiwan, and a steady increase of Hong Kong emigrants to Taiwan has been recorded in the past three years, from 2019 onwards. See "Another historical record for number of Hong Kong emigrants to Taiwan last year", *RFA*, 29 Jan 2022 (in Chinese), https://www.rfa.org/cantonese/ news/htm/tw-immigrant-01292022051209.html (last viewed 19 Sept 2022).

19 In his book about the 2019 protests, Antony Dapiran quoted Brian C.H. Fong, from a private conversation, that China was actually "dealing with a new, young nation, or at least with a group of people who considered themselves different from their sovereign" (Dapiran, 2020, p. 210).

2.1   *"Society of Social Movements" (Lee, 2021, p. 1)*

Several writers observe that a "protest culture" was built into the post-1997 Hong Kong society as a reaction to the fact that the promise of a high degree of political participation written into the Basic Law was never delivered. Following the large-scale protests in the summer of 2003, demands for democracy grew even stronger. The Chinese government announced in 2007 that universal suffrage for the election of the Chief Executive might be introduced ten years later, in 2017, and if that took place, for the Legislative Council in 2020 (Davis, 2021). Then in 2014 came the so-called "August 31 Decision", made by the National People's Congress Standing Committee, stating that for the 2017 Chief Executive election, two or three candidates would be nominated by a Nominating Committee which was similar to the existing Election Committee. These candidates, who would have to "love the country and love Hong Kong" (CCP-speak, meaning "pro-Beijing"), would have to receive support of more than half of the Election Committee before being presented for popular election. The process of the Legislative Council (LegCo) election in 2016 would remain the same as before, with a vague promise that following the election of the Chief Executive in 2017, a new system of universal suffrage for the LegCo elections would be developed with the approval of Beijing. So, seventeen years after the handover, democracy was still being stalled. This triggered off the announcement of "Occupy Central", which then gave way to the so-called "Umbrella Movement", which saw important thoroughfares in Admiralty/ Central, Mongkok and Causeway Bay being occupied for 79 days in 2014.

2.2   *Localism in the Protest Culture*

By this time, a new orientation in the protest culture has already set in. Long drawn-out resistance campaigns against the redevelopment of Lee Tung Street (2004–2010), the demolition of Star Ferry Pier and Queen's Pier (2006–7), the demolition of Tsoi Yuen Village and surrounding green land (generally named "Northeast-New Territories") for the construction of the High-Speed Railway linking Guangzhou, Shenzhen and Hong Kong (2009–2011) all called for the reclamation of history and identity by and for the common people. Together they proclaimed their right of participation in decision-making for the place they called "home", and they staunchly upheld civic ownership of public space against neoliberal commercialisation and statist projects. Local allegiance was paramount in this new generation of protesters, and so was effective action to defend their community.

In the campaigns defending Star Ferry Pier and Queen's Pier, and the movement against encroachment of Northeast-New Territories by the proposed High-Speed Railway, the Chinese state and state capital began to emerge as targets of popular movements which were fast gaining momentum. Moving into the second decade of the 21st century, this anti-Chinese sentiment became even clearer.

2.3   *"Hong Kong" vs "Chinese"*

In the summer of 2012, an unprecedented upsurge of teenage resistance flared up in the "Anti-Nationalist Education" (ANE) campaign. Led by Scholarism, a group consisting of high school students, and supported by a parents' concern group and other organisations like the PTU, the campaign targeted a proposed compulsory "Moral and National Education" subject in school, which the protesters accused of brainwashing by the Chinese state. After a series of protest marches, occupation of the Civic Square (officially the "East Wing Forecourt of the Central Government Offices" but christened "Civic Square" during this campaign), mass gatherings and concerts, and hunger strikes, the government backed down and the subject was withdrawn.[20] In hindsight, the Anti-Nationalist Education campaign was very much a small-scale rehearsal for the Umbrella Movement in 2014, minus the tear gas, triad assistance for the police (in the clearance of occupation in Mongkok), and arrests. Indeed, Joshua Wong and his group Scholarism did play a pivotal role again later in the 2014 Umbrella Movement.

Sandwiched between the 2012 Anti-Nationalist Education Movement and the 2014 Umbrella Movement was a lesser-known Anti-Putonghua as a Medium of Chinese (as a school subject) Campaign (APMC) (反普教中運動) (Choi, 2017). Apart from the youthfulness of the campaigners (secondary students in their mid-teens), a shared central tenet of the ANE and the APMC was the rejection of Chinese state (or rather, Party) domination. In the APMC, the emphasis on the unique, ethnic identity of Hong Kong, as exemplified in its use of Cantonese, was clear. This assertion of Hong Kong identity was not put at the forefront of the ANE, but by emphasising critical and independent thinking in education, this campaign was distancing Hong Kong education from that implemented in mainland China. The uniqueness of Hong Kong (or of what Hong Kong deserved) was clearly highlighted.

Thus, it comes as no surprise that in the 2014 Umbrella Movement, "debates and slogans about 'The Hong Kong nation/people deciding its destiny', 'subjectivity', 'agency', 'autonomy' (自主), 'self-determination' (自決), and 'masters

---

20   "Sequence of Events in the Anti-Brainwashing National Education Storm in Hong Kong",
      Voice of America, 3 Aug 2012, (in Chinese), https://www.voacantonese.com/a/hong-kong
      -events-against-national-education-review-20120803/1454655.html (in Chinese, last
      viewed on 16 Aug 2022).

of our own destiny' (命運自決)" were recurrent in the three occupied sites (Lee, 2022, p. 53). In the 2019 Movement, this dual theme of identity and self-determination was unmistakably clear.

Activism seemed to have quieted down after the Umbrella Movement. There was a brief but significant outburst, however, in February 2016. Spanning only one night, clashes between the police and protesters were nevertheless violent, by Hong Kong standards. This was the "Fish Ball Revolution" (or Mongkok Riots, depending on one's stance), so called because it had originated from activists defending the rights of vendors of a popular street food, fish balls, against official clearance. This incident marked a radicalisation of protest culture, and the emergence of calls by nascent localist groups for self-determination and autonomy. Not surprisingly, Chinese government organs reacted quickly with condemnation of the protesters as "separatist" and "terrorist".

Between 2012 and 2019 came also increasingly antagonistic protests against parallel traders in the border towns of Sheung Shui and Tuen Mun, termed "recovery campaigns". With large numbers of mainland Chinese visitors descending upon the city (about 6.7 mainland visitors for every local resident in 2018),[21] and the inconvenience caused by tourists and parallel traders who snapped up baby formula and other daily necessities to meet the demand that had grown out of toxic foodstuffs in China, many locals felt displaced (Laidler & Lee, 2014; Wan et al., 2016).[22] Then there is the daily legal quota (150) of Chinese immigrants, over which the Hong Kong government has no control. On the macro level, there has been a massive influx of Chinese state capital into Hong Kong since 1997, which, coupled with government land policy, drove up land prices and costs of living. These, together with growing income inequality and worsening livelihood, explain the xenophobic sentiments which coloured the "recovery campaigns".

These xenophobic sentiments were also present, though in a lesser way, in the 2019 Movement. The resounding call in 2019 was "Hong Kong is not China!" Here, however, it was not so much the Chinese people but the Chinese ruling power – the state and the CCP – and the autocracy and corruption they represented that the 2019 protesters were opposed to. The "Hong Kong" they

---

21   See "Facts and Statistics", Tourist Commission, 2022, for number of tourists (including those from mainland China) https://www.tourism.gov.hk/en/tourism-statistics-2018.php (last viewed 18 Aug 2022). For population figures, see "Population and Immigration", in *Hong Kong Yearbook*, Hong Kong Government, 2018, pp. 287–292, https://www.yearbook.gov.hk/2018/en/pdf/E18.pdf (last viewed 18 Aug 2022).

22   For the strained relationship between local residents and parallel traders as well as mainland tourists, see Laidler & Lee (2014), and Wan et al (2016).

were trying to defend was a society with the rule of law, a clean government, freedom, and democracy.

The pursuit of these values was an uphill battle. As we have seen above, the universal suffrage that has been promised in the Basic Law was denied. Not only that, but new measures were taken to make it even harder for members of the pro-democracy camp to get into the undemocratic system even if they wished. In 2016, the Electoral Affairs Commission announced that candidates who ran for elections to the LegCo must sign a declaration that he/she upheld the Basic Law and that he/she would pledge allegiance to the Hong Kong Special Administrative Region. The Commissioner reserved the right to decide whether the declaration of individual candidates was satisfactory. In the elections to LegCo of that year, six candidates, most of them young people from localist groups, were barred on grounds that their declarations were not genuine.[23] Then, after the elections, six elected pro-democracy lawmakers were disqualified on grounds that they did not stick to the given text in the swear-in ceremony.[24] Likewise, in 2018, three pro-democracy candidates were barred from the LegCo by-elections.[25] The club of disqualification was wielded to maximum capacity to squeeze the already narrow crevice leading to political participation. No wonder a political commentator wrote, in February 2018, these fateful words:

> A whole generation of young people is being dissuaded from participating in the formal political system, becoming ever more hostile toward it if not cynical ... It seems that the success of self-determination will depend on a broad-based mass movement, and this requires reaching out to the people and deep organisation, not just mobilisation for the occasional elections.[26]

The 'broad-based mass movement' did occur in 2019, and it reached out to a much greater number and a much wider social and age spectrum than anyone could have imagined, though sadly, it was crushed relentlessly. Dapiran's

---

23   Lam (2016).

24   Elson Tong, "4 more elected pro-democracy lawmakers to be ousted following Hong Kong court ruling", *Hong Kong Free Press*, 14 July 2017, https://hongkongfp.com/2017/07/14 /breaking-4-elected-pro-democracy-lawmakers-ousted-following-hong-kong-court-rul ing/ (last viewed 20 Aug 2022).

25   Kong (2018); "LegCo By-election: Another candidate barred from running", *The Standard*, 1 Feb 2018, https://www.thestandard.com.hk/breaking-news/section/4/102408/(Legco-by -election)-Another-candidate-barred-from-running, (last viewed 20 Aug 2022).

26   Kong (2018).

depiction of the younger generations of Hongkongers as "a new, young nation" holding completely different values from those of their sovereign was an accurate one. But their existence was not something that the autocratic, one-party CCP state could stomach. In the words of Stephen Vines: "China doesn't tolerate internationalism or diversity, so Hong Kong people being HongKongers need to be suppressed" (Vines, 2021, p. 101).

3   The 2019 Hong Kong Protests and the Changing World Order

The scale and intensity of the 2019 protests went way beyond everyone's imagination. The protest started like many others did in the past: open statements by various groups of co-signatories, legal assemblies, and peaceful protest marches with police's "letter of no objection", etc. But this time the police and government's response were totally out of proportion and the cycle of protests and suppression spiralled. Our interviewees reported being shocked by the heavy-handed tactics used by the riot police on 12 June, who fired tear gas indiscriminately at protesters, almost causing a fatal stampede in an enclosed building where they tried to seek shelter. Then, on 14 July, riot police chased and beat up protesters in a major shopping mall in Shatin, causing panic among trapped Sunday shoppers and restaurant patrons. The gravest injustice that remains unredressed until today is, of course, the collusion of the police and triad members in the vicious attack on passengers in Yuen Long station on 21 July. The brutal attack of passengers by the police in train compartments in Prince Edward station on 31 August is yet another unforgettable grievance. As reported by our interviewees, anger, shock, and a strong sense of injustice mobilised and intensified their actions, and this explained the rapid escalation of the Movement.

Two decades after the return of Hong Kong to Chinese sovereignty, we finally reached a point where China could no longer tolerate the degree of autonomy enjoyed by this city, unimaginable in other Chinese cities. China had devised the "One Country Two Systems" formula because Hong Kong was, and still is (though to a reduced extent) an important outpost for its economic expansion. But by the end of the 2010s, China decided to reign in this recalcitrant city with its protest culture. For the CCP rulers, this culture was even more intolerable because it influenced other Chinese cities, which began to imitate Hong Kong's social movements and grassroots organisations (Au, 2020). At the same time, the so-called "colour revolutions" in former East European countries, as well as revolts in Tibet, Xinjiang and the "Arab Spring" protests gave Beijing the jitters and heightened its concern for national security (Lee, 2022). The price for allowing Hong Kong autonomy now seemed too high.

Beijing had previously consented to pay this price because it had to rely on Hong Kong's help to build its new capitalism. With China becoming the second largest world economy, and with the ascendance of Xi Jinping in 2012, Beijing felt strong enough to clamp down on Hong Kong's autonomy. Further along this line, Au (2020) argued that China was no longer content to remain a second-rate world power subservient to the US, which, however, would not give up its hegemony. This set the stage in China's contest as manifested in the South China Sea dispute, the trade war and Hong Kong.

Lee (2022) argued from yet another angle. She pointed out that Beijing's performance-based legitimacy was undermined by the exhaustion of China's export-led economic growth since the 2008 global economic crisis which, in turn, was exacerbated by its overcapacity problem. It therefore had to intensify its global expansion, including Hong Kong, to strengthen its legitimacy internally. Whether Beijing had acted from a position of strength or out of a feeling of threat, or more likely, both, the 2019 protests clearly occurred at a moment when Beijing's relationships with the world were undergoing a drastic change. To be more precise, the 2019 protests occurred at a moment when, in Lee's words, "China's relation with the West had shifted from one of strategic engagement to one of strategic competition" (2022, p. 59). Au (2020) goes further to say that, when the HKSAR government suppressed the 2019 protests in the way it did, and when it followed Beijing's orders to undermine the rule of law and civil society Hong Kong once enjoyed, the interests of the West in Hong Kong and in China are also affected. So, a collision between the West and Beijing becomes unavoidable.

Video clips and on-site reporting of the massive and often principled and disciplined protests, as well as brutal police suppression transmitted real-time worldwide during that second half year of 2019 put Hong Kong on the global spotlight. Not only that, the 2019 Movement in Hong Kong actually "became the frontier of international conflicts", in Lee's words (2022, p. 67). It revealed the true face of China's expansionism, and the lengths it would go to exert and extend its autocratic rule. Relations between China and the world have already been changing, and "the combination of the fallout from the Hong Kong uprising and the pandemic has become a catalyst for changing attitudes towards the [People's Republic of China] – perhaps fundamentally ..." (Vines, 2021, p. 231).

4   Actors or Pawns in History?

In his book, *The Hong Kong Diaries*, the last British Governor of Hong Kong, Chris Patten (2022), recalled meeting a certain Professor Wu in 1994.[27] This is what Patten wrote:

> [Professor Wu] is pretty pessimistic about China and told me that in his view it will take many years for it to change. He also reckons that Hong Kong will have a tough time after 1997, though whether it will be wrecked will depend on how much people are prepared to fight for it. But what, I asked, will the communists do if people do fight for it? We both have an uneasy feeling that we know the answer. (pp. 201–202).

The conversation took place thirty years ago, and one gets goosebumps reading it now. Today, Hong Kong is wrecked, badly, if not totally. But the people did put up a good fight. In the stories we offer here, we see the bravery, determination, and depth of commitment they brought to this fight. We also see their sacrifices and hurt, physical and otherwise, that they had to bear. At the same time, we feel their sense of warmth and gratification when complete strangers offered unconditional help and support, and when the sense of community and solidarity among *their* people – the Hongkongers – manifested daily in those fateful months. Today we seem to know the answer Patten and Professor Wu came up with, and then we ask whether the fight was worth it after all.

There is the perennial question of whether (or how much) people could decide on their fate, or whether they are just pawns in the game of history. In the previous section, we attempted to put Hong Kong's resistance to the tyranny of the CCP state in the context of China's rise to power and its changing relationship with the world. Looking back, one sees that the iron fist would close in anyway, with China feeling confident enough in the 2010s to steer Hong Kong's "second return (to the motherland)".[28] It is equally clear, on the

---

27   We believe it was Professor Wu Ningkun, who co-wrote a memoir, *A Single Tear*. In this book, he documents the unimaginable suffering he and his family underwent in China, starting from the late 1950s all the way to the Cultural Revolution. See Wu & Li (1994).

28   In pro-Beijing circles, the talk of "the second return" came up after the passing of the National Security Law in July 2020. Compared to the "first return" in 1997, the "second return" signifies that all lingering "foreign influences" have been eliminated, and Hong Kong is firmly under the rule of China. See, for example, Chan Ging Lap, "Hong Kong Needs the Second Return", *on.cc.*, 25 June 2020. (in Chinese) https://hk.on.cc/hk/bkn/cnt /commentary/20200625/bkn-20200625000433631-0625_00832_001.html (last viewed 30 Aug 2022).

other hand, that people – "the new, young nation", in Dapiran's words, would fight back. The moot point is whether the fight has changed anything.

This is the sort of question to which no one can provide a certain answer. In this context, one recalls the "Tank Man" on Tiananmen Square in that fateful summer of 1989. Holding what looked like a plastic bag in one hand and standing in front of a line of moving tanks, the lone man played out the absurdity expressed in the Chinese idiom "the mantis trying to stop the chariot" (螳臂擋車). But, when the Tank Man photo circulated worldwide, it was the incredible courage which impressed the spectators instead. The Tank Man had not changed anything with his valiant act. The tanks rolled in anyway and the massacre took place, but the photo crystallised the human resolve against the brutality of the State's Army, despatched to crush its own people. The flicker of hope remains.

Let us come back to the 2019 fight in Hong Kong. As the international context changed, the Hong Kong protests were put on global spotlight, and the protesters themselves did contribute to this. Among other things, they made strenuous efforts to publicise the protests and to garner international support, the most notable attempt being crowdfunding to put up advertisements in up to ten countries on the eve of the G20 meeting in August 2019, all done within a miraculously short time. Those who worked on this "international front" were, together with the other participants of the Movement, "actors in the contention of our time", in the words of the researcher, Francis Lee (Lee, 2021).

Like the Tank Man, they seemed not to have changed anything. The Movement was crushed in any case, and thousands of protesters were jailed, many before trial with the term of imprisonment yet unknown. Many other Hong Kong people fled the city, mostly to the United Kingdom, Canada, Australia, and Taiwan. Hong Kong, as it was, seemed to have gone. But like the Tank Man photo, these stories will remain.

Recalling the waves of mass protests that had come to pass, a team member of ours said in early 2021, "It feels so strange. What was all swells and surges a year ago is now but the moon in the water." This book, alongside others, is written to preserve memories of those surges and swells. Our stories here obviously cannot stand up to the power of the state, what with its army, police, laws, courts, propaganda, and all. But our faith rests with telling those stories:

As a society, stories, plural, are the most valuable things we have. They enable us to connect and make sense of ourselves through time.[29]

In an era of anger, fear, despair, and confusion that sees no end, could there be more pressing matters?

---

29 Jeffrey Boakye, Introduction to "What an English Degree did to me by Tulip Siddiz, Sarah Waters and More", *The Guardian* (The Observer, Higher Education), 14 Aug 2022, https://www.theguardian.com/education/2022/aug/14/what-an-english-degree-did-for-me-earning-sunak-arts-humanities, (last viewed, 3 Sept 2022).

References

A group of local professionals. (2019). *Legal powers and monitoring of the Hong Kong Police* (in Chinese). https://bit.ly/3EwQYcg (no longer available).

Amnesty International. (2019, June 21). *How not to police a protest: Unlawful use of force by Hong Kong Police.* Hong Kong. Retrieved September 3, 2022, from https://www.amnesty.org/en/documents/asa17,0576/2019/en/.

Au, L. Y. (2020). *Hong Kong in revolt: The protest movement and the future of China.* London: Pluto Press.

Centre for Communication and Public Opinion Survey, The Chinese University of Hong Kong. (2020, May). *Research report on public opinion during the Anti-Extradition Bill (Fugitive Offenders Bill) Movement in Hong Kong.* http://www.com.cuhk.edu.hk/ccpos/en/pdf/202005PublicOpinionSurveyReport-ENG.pdf (last viewed, 9 Jan 2023).

Choi, P. K. (2017). Should the Chinese language be taught in Putonghua? Contested identities in post-1997 Hong Kong. *Asia Colloquia Papers, 7*(1), 1–19. https://ycar.apps01.yorku.ca/wp-content/uploads/2013/09/YCAR_ACP0701.pdf (last viewed 1 Oct 2022).

Dapiran, A. D. (2020). *City on fire: The fight for Hong Kong.* London: Scribe.

Davis, M. C. (2021). *Making Hong Kong China: The rollback of human rights and the rule of law.* Ann Arbor: Association for Asian Studies.

Hong Kong Public Opinion Research Institute. (2019, December 13). *Anti-extradition Bill Movement: People's public sentiment report.* Hong Kong. Retrieved September 3, 2022, from https://www.pori.hk/wp-content/uploads/2021/01/pcf_s3_ppt_v2_bilingual_cty.pdf.

Kong, T. G. (2018, January 31). Disqualified: How the gov't compromised Hong Kong's only free and fair election. *Hong Kong Free Press.* https://hongkongfp.com/2018/01/31/disqualified-hong-kong-govt-compromised-citys-free-fair-elections/ (last viewed, 9 Jan 2023).

Laidler, K. J., & Lee, M. (2014). Border trading and policing of everyday life in Hong Kong. In S. Pickering, & J. Ham (Eds.), *The Routledge handbook on crime and international migration* (pp. 316–328). London: Routledge.

Lam, O. (2016, August 5). Hong Kong election officials disqualify six legislative candidates for not being 'loyal' enough to China. *Global Voices.* https://globalvoices.org/2016/08/05/hong-kong-election-officials-disqualify-six-legislative-candidates-for-not-being-loyal-enough-to-china/ (last viewed 20 August 2022).

Lau, C. K. R. (2020). *Dark night in Yuen Long: My memories and those of others.* Hong Kong: Lau Chun Kong. (柳俊江《元朗黑夜：我的記憶和眾人的記憶》香港：柳俊江, 2020).

Lee, C. K. (2022). *Hong Kong: Global China's restive frontier.* London: Cambridge University Press.

Lee, L. F. F. (2021). *Actors in the contention of our time.* Hong Kong: Oxford University Press (China). (李立峰《時代的行動者》香港：牛津出版社[中國], 2021).

Lee, L. F. F., Yuen, S., Tang, G., & Cheng, E. W. (2019). Hong Kong's summer of uprising: From anti-extradition to anti-authoritarian protests. *The China Review, 19*(4), 1–32.

Ma, N. (2020). *Community of resistance: 2019 Anti-extradition movement in Hong Kong.* Taipei: Rivergauche/Walkers Cultural Enterprise Ltd. (馬嶽《反抗的共同體》台北：左岸文化/遠足文化事業股份有限公司, 2020).

Malcolm, X. (1992). *By any means necessary – Malcolm X speeches & writings* (2nd ed.). New York: Pathfinder Press.

Patten, C. (2022). *The Hong Kong Diaries.* London: Penguin Books.

Progressive Scholars Group. (2020). *Silencing millions: Unchecked violence of internationally recognized human rights by the Hong Kong Police Force.* Hong Kong. Retrieved September 3, 2022, from https://www.docdroid.net/oEA2Bhy/silencingmillions-text-final-pdf.

Stott, C., Ho, L., Radburn, M., Chan, Y. T., Kyprianides, A., & Morales, P. S. (2020). Patterns of 'disorder' during the 2019 protests in Hong Kong: Policing, social identity, intergroup dynamics, and radicalization. *Policing: A Journal of Policy and Practice, 14*(4), 815–835.

UN Human Rights Committee. (2022, July 27). *Concluding observations on the fourth periodic report of Hong Kong, China.* Geneva: UN Human Rights Committee. Retrieved October 1, 2022, from https://www.cmab.gov.hk/doc/en/documents/policy_responsibilities/the_rights_of_the_individuals/CCPR_C_CHN-HKG_CO_4_49295_E.pdf.

Vines, S. (2021). *Defying the dragon: Hong Kong and the world's largest dictatorship.* London: Hurst & Co.

Wan, T. Y. T., Chiew, T. H. T., Cheung, T. P. H., Wong, F. K. Y., Tsoi, C., & Laidler, K. J. (2016). Parallel trading and its implications for policing the border. *Social Transformations in Chinese Societies, 12*(1), 77–96. https://doi.org/10.1108/STICS-05-2016-004 (last viewed 9 Jan 2023).

Wu, N., & Li, Y. (1994). *A single tear: A family's persecution, love and endurance in Communist China.* New York: Back Bay Books.

Index